BORGES, THE JEW

SUNY series in Latin American and Iberian Thought and Culture

---

Jorge J. E. Gracia and Rosemary Geisdorfer Feal, editors

BORGES, THE JEW

ILAN STAVANS

STATE UNIVERSITY OF NEW YORK PRESS

Published by
State University of New York Press, Albany

Printed in the United States of America

For information, contact
State University of New York Press, Albany, NY
www.sunypress.edu

Production, Laurie D. Searl
Marketing, Michael Campochiaro

Library of Congress Cataloging-in-Publication Data

Names: Stavans, Ilan, author.
Title: Borges, the Jew / Ilan Stavans.
Description: Albany : State University of New York Press, [2016] | Series: SUNY series in Latin American and Iberian thought and culture | Includes bibliographical references and index.
Identifiers: LCCN 2015036569 | ISBN 9781438461434 (hardcover : alk. paper) | ISBN 9781438461441 (e-book)
Subjects: LCSH: Borges, Jorge Luis, 1899–1986—Criticism and interpretation. | Judaism and literature. | Jews in literature.
Classification: LCC PQ7797.B635 Z9183 2016 | DDC 868/.6209—dc23
LC record available at http://lccn.loc.gov/2015036569

10 9 8 7 6 5 4 3 2 1

I feel a contentment in defeat.

—"Deutsches Requiem" (1946)

CONTENTS

PREFACE

OUTSIDER

It is perhaps ironic that Jorge Luis Borges (1899–1986), a lifelong lover of *orillas*, the margin, the edge, is now a staple of Western Civilization, one of its spokespersons, his imagination having looped from a freak's show in the remote Buenos Aires of the first half of the twentieth century to in irreplaceable ingredient to understand the postmodern condition.

Outsider is an English word often used in Spanish, where it has a unique connotation: loner, renegade, iconoclast. Borges doesn't use it in his Buenos Aires conference "The Argentine Writer and Tradition" (1951), where he talked of Jews as innovators because they "do not feel bound" by any devotion to culture, being at once insiders and unattached observers. The same might be said of him, not only in regard to Argentina but in general: he looks at things, borrowing from Spinoza, *sub specie aeternitatis*, as if from beyond.

Another irony: Borges's oeuvre is relatively short, yet it has generated an endless river of ink. That contrast is apparent in my personal library, where his stories, essays, poetry, and studies on literature make a short section compared with the endless exegesis they have fostered. (A large portion of the library is also made of translations of his work into all sorts of languages.) Why then add yet another volume to that abundance?

My answer: *Borges, the Jew* highlights an aspect dear to me—his relentless desire (not to be confused with envy) to claim, as part of his self, a Jewishness he found in books, in idols such as Baruch Spinoza, in an overall attitude, at once reverential and subversive, toward God, life, and the intellect. By his account, none of that Jewishness was in his blood; he desperately sought to trace it in genealogical terms yet failed in the endeavor. In response, he simply imagined himself a Jew.

This, therefore, is an act of repayment on my part, for, as a Jew and a Latin American, thanks to Borges I have come to understand, in probing ways, how to appreciate the confines, the edges of my own self.

Ever since I began reading him, in Spanish in my native Mexico in my early twenties, after a long sojourn away from home, I haven't stopped. Or I should say: rather than reading, I have been rereading, even memorizing him. By now (I have turned fifty), Borges is a compass. I see through his mind's eye. My intension in this slim volume is to reflect on his interest in Jewish motifs as seen in his life and work, offering some detailed, Talmudic look at a catch phrase, a character, a plotline. I myself have learned what it means to be a Jew through his meditations on time, dreams, *doppelgänger,* and language as a whole.

Indeed, I have not only understood what my tradition is—from the Bible to Kafka, from Kabbalah and Sh. Y. Agnon to the creation of the State of Israel; I have also constructed by own vision of the divine as a result. That vision, in an uncompromising way, is about being an outsider.

I like being foreign.

Now I want to explain how Borges metamorphosed himself, against all odds, into *un judío honorario,* an honorary Jew. My survey, hence, is at once personal and historical. I have neither interest nor patience in disengaged scholarship; the affairs of the heart and the mind matter to me in intimate fashion. My principal argument is that Borges found Jewishness to be a key to entering and exiting the world, a way of reading, or better, a relentless desire to translate other literatures in order to make them feel like home. Borges the Jew is also Borges the translator.

I have come to recognize that an argument, to be convincing, doesn't need to be linear. It will take the reader no effort to realize that that this volume is deliberately fractured. In *Borges, the Jew* there are biographical portions that have a linear structure and address Borges's intellectual odyssey; there are also sections in which I switch modes, maybe dramatically, focusing my interest in a particular poem by Borges, in translation (say that of William Faulkner's *The Wild Palms*) or in *una afinidad*, a shared interest. I've never been attracted to books that give the reader what the reader wants; instead, I long for the ones that surprise us, that teach to want something else.

Part I looks at Borges's quest to find Jewish ancestors in his genealogy. Part II explores his reaction to Nazism and the Holocaust as well as to the creation of the State of Israel and Part III the Jewish motifs in his work. These sections place his career in historical context.

The next three sections, again with a decisively different tenor (less pompous, more personal), have language as their leitmotif. Part IV meditates on Borges as a translator and on translation as a favorite Jewish pastime—or, stated in a different way, on translation as the *raison d'être* of Jews. Let me qualify this statement. Since the destruction of the Second Temple of Jerusalem in 70 CE and until the creation of the State of Israel in 1948, Jewish life in the diaspora was—and still is—transient. That is, homelessness is its essential feature. Being uprooted, being a perennial guest, pushed Jews to focus on the text (the Torah, the *Talmud*, *Mishna*, and *Guemara*, literature in general) as a kind of portable homeland. Words, sentences, paragraphs, pages, the worlds they conjure, the interpretation they elicit justifies Jew existence.

Part V looks specifically at movie subtitles as a form of impostorship and wonders if ghosts understand each other. Borges loved ghost stories. ("The Monkey's Paw," by W. W. Jacobs, was among his favorites.) I nurture the belief that he saw himself as a ghost. And diaspora Jews, too. At any rate, in the coda, I compare several English-language renditions of

"*Borges y yo*," then wrap up the volume with a disquisition on a personal debt I owe to Borges, whom I see as my Virgil.

In sum, these last three sections constitute an alternative roadmap. They aren't an analysis, chronological in organization, of Borges's life and oeuvre. Instead, they engage, and even polemicize, with the idea of the Jew as "inhabiting" the text. I see them as my way to root him in my own *weltanschauung*, which I built in response—even and against—my lifelong career as his reader. Indeed, Borges to me is a home.

Is character fate? Borges didn't endorse this ancient Greek principle, on which entire tragedies were built. His character wasn't defiant; instead, he approached reality rationally, by which I also mean cautiously. Life, in his view, was a series of accidents. In "A History of the Echoes of a Name" (1955), he quotes Martin Buber, in his book *Between Man and Man* (1948), as saying that "to live is to enter the strange house of the spirit, whose floor is the chessboard on which we play an unknown and unavoidable game against a changing and sometimes frightening opponent."

I don't know if there is a Jewish approach to life but it does strike me that, if there is such a thing, it would indeed be a game played against a mysterious, out-of-this-world opponent: oneself.

PART I

YO, JUDÍO

If I am not one of Thy repetitions or errata . . .

—"The Secret Miracle" (1943)

Throughout his life, Borges was overwhelmed by a strange feeling of unworthiness. He was, he claimed, unworthy of friendship, love, and public attention. The more he achieved, the more puzzled he was by the towering praise that had descended on him. And he kept on waiting for the day when people would finally recognize how mistaken they had been about his genius. This might be seen as an excess of modesty; it could also be equated with a complex Jews are often linked to: self-deprecation.

Borges wasn't an aristocrat, although often he behaved as such. And even though his genealogical connection with the *soldados* in Argentina on his mother's side of the family is ethereal, his eulogies to them are defined by envy. Simply put, Borges refurbished his background, making it look more distinguished than it was; or more suitable to the ethos that defines a life spent with too many books around and too little adventure. Needless to say, this enhancement of one's own heritage, this falsification of the self, is a common trait in the Hispanic world, where *las apariencias engañan*, nothing is as it appears.

"I spent a great deal of my boyhood indoors," he wrote in a profile called "An Autobiographical Essay," published in *The New Yorker*, in the September 19, 1970, issue:

> Having no childhood friends, my sister and I invented two imaginary companions, named, for some, reason or other, Quilos and The Windmill. (When they finally bored us, we told our mother that they had died.) I was always very nearsighted and wore glasses, and I was rather frail.[1]

One of Borges's grandfathers, Francisco Borges Lafinur, had fought at the Battle of Caseros against the tyrant Juan Manuel de Rosas; he died in the Battle of La Verde, which was part of General Bartolomé Mitre's failed armed uprising against Domingo Faustino Sarmiento. What killed him were two bullets shot from a Remington rifle, the first time this weapon had ever been used in Argentina. This lineage of military men instrumental in the shaping of the Argentine Republic, he wrote in his diary, "may account for my yearning after that epic destiny which my gods denied me, no doubt wisely." This line signals Borges's unworthiness. It clearly shows how he saw himself for what *he was not* and how he used literature to impersonate that absence—to become the warrior he could never be.

Borges's paternal grandmother, Fanny Haslam, was an Englishwoman with a Quaker past. More important, she was a great reader. Her Spanish was fluent but poor; her English, on the other hand, was hypnotizing. In it she fell in love with her favorite authors: Arnold Bennett, Galsworthy, Dickens, and Thackeray; and she also introduced her grandchild to the beauties of the English language. Thanks in large part to her, Borges grew up in both English and Spanish. He did most of his early readings in Shakespeare's tongue, including *Don Quixote*, which, years later, upon rereading it in the original, seemed to him like a second-rate translation.

Again, the feeling of unworthiness. Borges's sense of possessing a masked identity is traceable to his philo-Semitism: his love of Jews. His genealogical tree doesn't show any Semitic lineage. But he longed for one. In a poem written in 1967, celebrating the triumphant Six Day War in which Israel defended itself against its Arab enemies, he wondered if Israel, as an emblem, could be found in his genealogy. Indeed, he faithfully searched throughout his entire life for a trace of Jewish blood in his ancestry. This is poignantly clear in a brief essay called "*Yo, judío*," whose historical value is decisive in understanding Borges's interest in things Jewish. Over the years, that interest, in its different facets, and with various degrees of success, has been explored by academics such as Edna Aizenberg, Saúl Sosnowski, and Jaime Alazraki. Herein the first paragraph of the essay, included in *Jorge Luis Borges: Selected Non-Fictions* (1999), in Eliot Weinberger's English translation:

> Like the Druzes, like the moon, like death, like next week, the distant past is one of those things that can enrich ignorance. It is infinitely malleable and agreeable, far more obliging than the future and far less demanding of our efforts. It is the famous season favored by all mythologies.

"I, a Jew" appeared in the April 1934 issue of the Buenos Aires magazine *Megáfono*. (Should the translation be "I, the Jew"?) It is among the least known essays by Borges, who saw it as an orphan piece, never collecting it in *Other Inquisitions* or any of his nonfiction volumes. However, it has always been available in Spanish in one form or another, and it surfaced briefly in English in an American anthology published by E. P. Dutton called *Borges: A Reader* (1981), edited by Emir Rodríguez Monegal and Alastair Reid, and in Weinberger's *Selected Non-Fictions*. The essay continues:

> Who has not, at one point or another, played with thoughts of his ancestors, with the prehistory of his flesh and blood? I have done so many times, and many times it has not displeased me to think of myself as Jewish. It is an idle hypothesis, a frugal and sedentary adventure that harms no one, not even the name of Israel, as my Judaism is wordless, like the songs of Mendelssohn. The magazine *Crisol* [*Crucible*], in its issue of January 30, has decided to gratify this retrospective hope; it speaks of my "Jewish ancestry, maliciously hidden" (the participle and the adverb amaze and delight me).

Borges reacted with enviable concentration, even stalwart conviction, to an accusation, made in 1934 by the magazine *Crisol*, that he was indeed a Jew. The accusation came from an anti-Semitic faction of the Argentine intelligentsia and had as an objective to discredit Borges in public opinion. He, in turn, took the accusation as a compliment.

At the time of the publication of "*Yo, judío*," Argentina, in what proved to be a pattern throughout the century, was ruled by the military. In 1933, *Megáfono* had devoted a full issue to Borges, who was regarded locally as what the Nicaraguan poet Rubén Darío once described, in general terms, as "*un raro*"—a Wildean dandy, an Europeanized auteur infatuated with metaphysics and prone to an obtuse vocabulary. As a response to the *Megáfono* festschrift, the right-wing, nationalist periodical *Crisol*, also published in Buenos Aires, attacked Borges for hiding his "Israelite" origins. "*Yo, judío*," his brave and unapologetic response to *Crisol*, pointed out, in the measured prose that was to become his trademark, a deep desire to find the missing link in his ancestry—the Jew in the mirror. The essay continues:

> Borges Acevedo is my name. Ramos Mejía, in a note to the fifth chapter of Rosas and His time, lists

> the family names in Buenos Aires at that time in order to demonstrate that all, or almost all, "come from Judeo-Portuguese stock." "Acevedo" is included in the list: the only supporting evidence for my Jewish pretensions until this confirmation in *Crisol.* Nevertheless, Captain Honorario Acevedo undertook a detailed investigation that I cannot ignore. His study notes that the first Acevedo to disembark on this land was the Catalan Don Pedro de Azevedo in 1728: landholder, settler of "Pago de los Arroyos," father and grandfather of cattle ranchers in that province, a notable who figures in the annals of the parish of Santa Fe and in the documents of the history and the Viceroyalty—an ancestor, in short, irreparably Spanish.
>
> Two hundred years and I can't find the Israelite; two hundred years and my ancestor still eludes me.
>
> I am grateful for the stimulus provided by *Crisol*, but hope is dimming that I will ever be able to discover my link to the Table of the Breads and the Sea of Bronze; to Heine, Gleizer, and the ten *Sefiroth*; to Ecclesiastes and Chaplin.

The final section of "*Yo, judío*" is emphatic. In it Borges establishes, once and for all, his unquestionable loyalty. In a country such as Argentina where anti-Semitism has been present from the second half of the nineteenth century onward, which marked the arrival of poor, Yiddish-speaking immigrants from Eastern Europe, whose landing was sometimes greeted with animosity, to outbursts of historical proportions like the labor unrest known as *Semana Trágica* in 1919, in which Jews were a prime target, and the terrorist attack against the Jewish Community Center in Buenos Aires on July 18, 1994—events about which I will talk at more length—Borges made a commitment to connect with the Jewish community in Buenos Aires.

> Statistically, the Hebrews were few. What would we think of someone in the year 4000 who uncovers people from San Juan province everywhere? Our inquisitors seek out Hebrews, but never Phoenicians, Garamantes, Scythians, Babylonians, Persians, Egyptians, Huns, Vandals, Ostrogoths, Ethiopians, Illyrians, Paphlagonians, Sarmatians, Medes, Ottomans, Berbers, Britons, Libyians, Cyclopes, or Lapiths. The nights of Alexandria, of Babylon, of Carthage, of Memphis, never succeeded in engendering a single grandfather; it was only to the tribes of the bituminous Dead Sea that this gift was granted.[2]

In the context of Argentine letters, and, by extension, in Hispanic intellectual circles, Borges is a *rara avis*. No other non-Jewish author from the region addresses Jewish themes with the depth and complexity of the Argentine. The question, one wonders, is why. How is it than in an area where *lo judío* is often met with *lo anti-judío*, an ecosystem in which Jews have thrived for more than a century and a half yet have also met with a persistent, unabated anti-Semitic animus, comes along so influential and visionary a figure?

The answer, perhaps, is that quality comes from contest. To be opposed gives literature a purpose.

Post Scriptum: "Bituminous" (in Spanish, *bituminoso*)—who else uses such word?

Through Borges's personal journey, one is able to get a sharp picture of the fragile status of Jews in the Hispanic world. As a result of his exposure to the immediate surroundings in Buenos Aires, Borges was less attracted to the Sephardim than to the Ashkenazi culture of the Yiddish-speaking immigrants and their descendants. These immigrants arrived at the River Plate in the last couple of decades of the nineteenth century. He maintained closed ties with a handful of urbane, forward-looking intellectuals, among them his tutor Alberto Gerchunoff (1884–1950), considered the grandfather of Jewish Latin American letters with his collection of vignettes *The Jewish Gauchos of the Pampas*, originally published in 1910 as a celebration of Argentina's first hundred years of independence.

Borges's Jewish education was far more cosmopolitan than most Jews received at the time, or, for that matter, than they do today, not only in Argentina. He learned about Jews from books. While still young, he read James Joyce (whose character Leopold Bloom struck him as emblematic of "*el judío errante*," the "Wandering Jew") and Franz Kafka, a writer that inspired him to such extent that he translated him into Spanish and for decades was among his first, and only, promoters in the Spanish-speaking world. Gustav Meyrink's German novel *The Golem* (1914) also left a deep impression. The Hassidic tales compiled by Martin Buber exercised a fascination for him. At different points in his life, he even expressed interest in learning ancient Hebrew. (He eventually settled for other ancient languages, including Anglo-Saxon.)

Here, I will make a detour to explore Jewish literature in Argentina. At the time of Borges's death, the country's Jewish community comprised a population of approximately 220,000. In contrast with the United States, Israel, France, and the former Soviet Union, this number is minuscule. Yet in the Hispanic world (including Spain and the Caribbean Basin), in which they totaled 450 million, it was the biggest, most vigorous concentration of Jews, and in Latin America alone it was the leader in size, followed by, in descending order, Brazil, Mexico, and Colombia.

The Ashkenazi population of Latin America arrived, cumulatively, roughly between 1880 and 1930, so by the time Borges came of age, Jews, mostly poor and uneducated, were a fixture in Argentinean society. Prior to this wave of immigration, another one across the Atlantic into the Spanish-language regions had taken place: thousands of *marranos*, New Christians, and crypto-Jews had arrived from Portugal, the Netherlands, and Northern Africa in the colonial era. They had also escaped from Spain directly, where persecution and forced conversion under the fist of the Holy Inquisition made life miserable incrementally since the thirteenth century, a process that culminated in the edict of expulsion of 1492. But for a variety of reasons the slow disappearance of these crypto-Jews, and of the New Christians that came at the same time, was all but consummated when the Yiddish-language *shtetl* dwellers made it to the same landscape. Argentina in particular was a magnet for large-scale philanthropists and organizations imbued in the project of the resettlement of Jews out of Europe.

The French benefactor Baron Maurice de Hirsch, as well as the *Alliance Israélite universelle*, put immense resources into the objective of making the Pampas a suitable habitat—by means of socialist agricultural communes—for poor Jews escaping pogroms in Poland, Lithuania, and Ukraine. The early immigrants, thus, were located in rural milieus where gaucho life prevailed. This explains the lore of the Jewish gaucho at the turn of the nineteenth century. However, life in the countryside only lasted one, at the most two, generations. The Jewish newcomers and their children slowly moved, en masse, to urban centers, especially to Buenos Aires. By the thirties, the majority of Jews were already not only fluent in Spanish but also active in Argentine society. Still, anti-Jewish sentiment, a fixture in Latin America since the arrival of the Spanish *conquistadores* and the Catholic missionaries, remained rampant, and to this day it refuses to vanish altogether.

I mentioned Alberto Gerchunoff a couple of paragraphs ago. He is considered the father of Jewish literature in Latin America, an imposing figure whose oeuvre serves as a map to understand the vicissitudes in Argentina's intellectual life in the first half of the twentieth century. Before Gerchunoff, one can find sketches, poems, vignettes, and chronicles of immigrant life, written by Jewish refugees in Russian, Polish, Hebrew, Yiddish, and at times in a rudimentary Spanish. He believed Argentina was a "*país de advenimiento*," a country of accession where Jews would be able to finally live without hatred in the Southern Cone. Gerchunoff's life and craft have to be understood in the context of the history of Jewish immigration to Argentina.

In 1891, when Gerchunoff was seven, his father traveled from Russia to the Pampas, and the family followed him. Agriculture and cattle raising were the jobs designated for the *shtetl* dwellers, and hard labor was their lot. As expressed in his 1914 autobiography *Entre Ríos, My Country*, published posthumously in 1950, Gerchunoff admired the capacity for hard work of his fellow Argentines. His family was first stationed in the colony of Moisés Ville, but when his father was brutally killed by a gaucho, or Argentine cowboy, they moved to the Rajíl colony. This tragic event and Gerchunoff's later adventures in the new settlement were the inspiration for his early work.

One of the admirable things about Gerchunoff is his multilingualism. Language, after all, is the basic vehicle by which any newcomer must begin to adapt to the new country. Most immigrants improvised a "survival" Spanish during their first Argentine decade, but in Gerchunoff's case, as a child not only did he learn to speak perfect Spanish, but by 1910, at the age of twenty-six, his prose was setting a linguistic and narrative standard. Reading him today, we discover in his writing stylistic forms that were later developed by his followers, among them Borges.

Simultaneously, Gerchunoff's brief biographical sketches of such writers as Sholem Aleichem, Miguel de Unamuno, James Joyce, Max Nordau, and I. L. Peretz, which appeared in newspapers and magazines, and his deep and careful readings of British writers such as G. K. Chesterton, H. G. Wells, and Rudyard Kipling, influenced future artistic generations on the River Plate. Even if he did not fully belong to the popular *modernista* movement budding at the turn of the century in Latin America, many moderns welcomed his literature. The Cuban activist José Martí, the Mexican sonneteer Manuel Gutiérrez Nájera, and other *modernistas* dreamed of reviving all literatures written in Spanish. So did Gerchunoff, although he did not quite share the aesthetic and political values of these contemporaries.

His objective was to help Jews become Argentines, to be like everyone else. Following his death, after having composed some two dozen books and innumerable articles, he was praised by Borges himself as "*the writer of le mot juste*." Such a distinction, one should add, is seldom awarded to an immigrant. I can think of only a few others who have achieved it, among them Vladimir Nabokov, Joseph Brodsky, and Joseph Conrad.

It isn't common for traditions to have clearly defined genealogies. This happens in the Jewish literature of Latin America because of its short history: in tangible terms, it only started in the early twentieth century. This is if one ignores *converso* manifestations in the colonial period. This is a common practice—and, in fact, necessarily—because these manifestations, which align themselves in the shadow, concealing the hidden self, don't align themselves in full with Jewish tradition. Also, this artificial divide is the result of the parting of historical waters: the Sephardic and Ashkenazic literary traditions haven't been seen as a unit until rather recently; in previous epochs, they were perceived as parallel lines that never intersected.

Gerchunoff's role is not unlike that of Mendele Mokher Sforim, aka Sholem Yankev Abramovitch, the *zayde* of the Yiddish literary tradition. Although the two belong to two different worlds and even different languages, both managed to create a sense of literary tradition and continuity absent before. Mendele was considered by Sholem Aleichem to be the grandfather of Yiddish letters, as Gerchunoff became a cultural mentor and compass for later Jewish writers in Argentina such as Gerardo Mario Goloboff, Mario Szichman, Alicia Steimberg, and Isidoro Blaisten. In fact, the comparison is a clue to the linguistic reality the Argentine had to face: by writing in Spanish, he subscribed to the chain of Spanish and South American letters; Yiddish, the language of most of the immigrants, was left behind after he began publishing, and replaced by Spanish, a cosmopolitan, secular vehicle. Indeed, one has to consider that very few Jewish writers, even if they had some knowledge of Yiddish, could write anything beyond a crude transliterated version.

That's why some, including Gerchunoff himself and successors such as Mario Szichman, used transliterated Yiddish in dialogue. Besides, a Yiddish-reading audience today is practically nonexistent. Mendele found Yiddish the appropriate vehicle for communication with his people; for Gerchunoff, it was Spanish, the idiom of "exile," that turned them into "normal" citizens of Argentina. The two were equally celebrated as speakers of the collective soul.

During his youth, Gerchunoff had an acquaintance, Leopoldo Lugones, a representative of the *modernistas* in Argentina and paternalistically philo-Jewish and pro-immigrant, who gained access for him to *La Nación*, a very influential newspaper in Buenos Aires. Yet Lugones's last, sour years and his own ideological odyssey are symbolic of the attitude of Argentina as a whole toward the Jews: at first a socialist and a liberal, in his mature years and up until his suicide in 1938 he was a fascist and a nationalist. By then the Jews, "alien" people in his eyes, were unacceptable to him as equals because they represented the unwelcome outsider.

This hostility has its counterpart. Take the example of Rubén Darío, the *modernista* par excellence and famous Nicaraguan poet who in 1888 wrote *Azul . . .* (Blue), a book whose impact on Hispanic letters was equivalent to that of T. S. Eliot's *The Waste Land* on English poetry. Darío saw the Jews as appealing citizens, paradoxically both symbolic of an eternal voyage and deeply rooted in the Argentine soil. In a beautiful poem entitled "Song to Argentina," he celebrated the biblical heritage and bucolic present of the citizens of Entre Rios and Santa Fe. Here is a rough, free translation of one of its stanzas:

Sing Jews of La Pampa!
Young men of rude appearance,
sweet Rebeccas with honest eyes,
Reubens of long locks,
patriarchs of white,
dense, horselike hair.
Sing, sing old Sarahs
and adolescent Benjamins
with the voice of our heart:
"We have found ZION!"[3]

The very same tone is to be found in the twenty-six stories collected by Gerchunoff in *The Jewish Gauchos*, the book to which he owes his fame, a parade of Spanish-speaking but stereotypical Jewish men and women from Eastern Europe adapting to the linguistic and cultural reality of the southern hemisphere. The autonomous narratives that make up every chapter, some better than others, recreate life, tradition, and hard labor in this "new *shtetl*" across the Atlantic. The focus is on relations between Jews and gentiles, the passion to maintain their Jewish religion yet understand and assimilate new customs.

What is most striking about the book to today's reader is the political ideology it professes. Nineteen ten, one should know, was the centenary of Argentina's independence, and Gerchunoff meant his text to be a celebration of the nation's friendly, tolerant, and multiethnic spirit. He had moved to Buenos Aires in 1895 and, beginning in August 1902, contributed regularly to many newspapers, among them *La Nación*. Even after the tragic loss of his father, he stubbornly went on believing that Argentina was a true paradise. He saw the province of Entre Ríos and the cosmopolitan Buenos Aires as a diasporic "holy land" of sorts where the contribution of the Jews would always be welcome in shaping the national culture and where all manifestations of anti-Semitism would ultimately vanish. Such optimism flourished for only a single generation. It evaporated even faster than the hatred it stood against.

In the short story "Camacho's Wedding Feast," part of *The Jewish Gauchos of the Pampas*, Gerchunoff describes the sorrows of a Jewish family when their daughter, about to be married off to a rich Jew, is suddenly carried off by her gentile lover, Camacho, on the very day of the wedding. To be sure, the motif of the stolen bride is universal, having been used by Boccaccio, Federico García Lorca, and Charles Dickens.

Yet note Gerchunoff's selection of the Argentine character's name: Camacho was also part of the cast of *Don Quixote of La Mancha*. With all its literary echoes, the author of *The Jewish Gauchos* is able to create a tale in a style that reminds us of oral storytelling. He does it by having a tête-à-tête with the reader and by shaping an unpretentious, colloquial prose that foreshadows the experimental techniques yet to come in Latin America. Here's the illuminating passage:

> Well, as you can see, my patient readers, there are fierce, arrogant Gauchos, wife-stealers and Camachos, as well as the most learned and honorable of rabbinical scholars in the little Jewish colony where I learned to love the Argentine sky and felt a part of its wonderful earth. This story I've told—with more detail than art—is a true one, just as I'm sure the original story of Camacho's feast is true. May I die this instant if I've dared to add the slightest bit of invention to the marvelous story.
>
> I'd like very much to add some verses—as was done to the original Camacho story—but God has denied me that talent. I gave you the tale in its purest truth, and if you want couplets, add them yourself in your most gracious style. Don't forget my name, however—just as our gracious Master Don Miguel de

> Cervantes Saavedra remembered the name of Cide Hamete Benegeli and gave him all due credit for the original Camacho story.
>
> And if the exact, accurate telling of this tale has pleased you, don't send me any golden doubloons—here, they don't even buy bread and water. Send me some golden drachmas or, if not, I'd appreciate a carafe of Jerusalem wine from the vineyards my ancestors planted as they sang the praises of Jehovah.[4]

Three things are evident from this passage: the author's deep and honest love for his new country, Argentina; his parody of *Don Quixote*; and his sense of tradition, both Jewish and Hispanic. This last is crucial: by referring to Cervantes, Gerchunoff, as a member of a cultural minority, nevertheless placed himself in the grand tradition of Hispanic letters.

While on the one hand he wanted to forge a link with the great master of Renaissance Spain, on the other he sought to relate himself to the Jewish past by referring to such biblical symbols as the wine "from the vineyards my ancestors planted as they sang the praises of Jehovah." Thus, two paths intersect in *The Jewish Gauchos*, and the encounter is dynamic and reciprocal. The Jews of Gerchunoff's community of Entre Ríos behave like gauchos, and the gauchos, in turn, inherit from the Jews a set of ethical values. Writing at the moment of Argentina's first centennial, the author sings to a new communion and to a fresh, hopeful love affair. This glorification of assimilation is puzzling.

As critic Naomi Lindstrom, in *Jewish Issues in Argentine Literature* (1989), claims: "The [novel] assumes that the long-standing Hispanic population of Argentina are the hosts, whereas the new Argentines coming from Eastern European Jewry are guests who must take care not to disrupt preexisting national life with their alien ways."[5] The goal for Gerchunoff's patriotism is to dream of a democratic society where Jews share and actually contribute to the new culture. But was that the goal of the Jewish immigrants as a whole?

Within a few years after 1910, things turned sour in Argentina. And Gerchunoff's perception of the country as a new "Zion" was not left unchallenged. On the contrary, it was opposed and even repudiated by Jewish intellectuals and literati. More than that, his response to a major crisis for the Jews in Argentina was regarded as disappointing for a figure of his stature. Anti-Semitism reached its height in 1919 with the *Semana Trágica,* the tragic week, an explosion of xenophobic fear that amounted to a full-blown pogrom with numerous injured and dead. (David Viñas, a Jewish novelist born ten years after the tragedy, made use of this sad event, a reminder that the heart of the Americas was not untouched by the same hatred left behind in the old continent, in a novel published in 1966.)

The intensification of negative feelings toward the Jews, generated by a wave of nationalism during the first administration of Hipólito Irigoyen (1916–1922), contributed to profound disappointment and skepticism regarding the future of a pluralistic society in Argentina. Though deeply affected, Gerchunoff did not publicly comment on the event. His silence was taken as a sign of self-criticism as well as cowardly passivity: some thought he might have come to the conclusion that assimilation was impossible in a country with such profound anti-Semitic feelings. The public would have to wait for a coherent statement. Of course, Gerchunoff was no politician; yet in Latin America the opinions of intellectuals are often the only channels through which deep political and ethical concerns are expressed.

Leonardo Senkman, in his study *Jewish Identity in Argentine Literature* (1983), discusses the various essays Gerchunoff wrote to articulate and explain his ideas. In response to Adolf Hitler's ascendancy to power in Germany, Gerchunoff's arguments finally became clear in his brief prologue to an Argentine edition of Ludwig Lewisohn's *Rebirth: A Book of Modern Jewish Thought* (1937). Speaking out against a restriction imposed on

Jewish immigration by the Argentine government that limited the quota of immigrants to at least one-third of the number in previous years, he openly defended the right of the Jews to live anywhere at any time without prohibitions.

It is not difficult to feel in his words a fear of the growth of anti-Semitic literature at the time of the invigorated Nationalist Party, which supported Irigoyen, and its call for the expulsion or even annihilation of all Jews in Argentina. Yet Gerchunoff's general passivity is palpable when placed in relation to the Zionist struggle for an independent Jewish state in Palestine that was taking place in those years. Though angry, he never advocated any kind of Jewish collective self-assertion. I translate:

> What should we do? Jews and Argentines, we can protest, fight, expose the hidden goals of the policy of cowardice and crime. And it would be proper to set a foundation for the right of the Jew to life, the right of the Jew to go on living exactly in the same place he was born or where he was left by fate, in the name of the following evidence:
>
> (1) No effort in history to get rid of the Jewish element has been successful, precisely because the Jew, anywhere, is irreplaceable when he performs on the stage of the human spirit, and ineradicable even when one tries to dissimulate his physical presence by means of alien dicta forced on him. . . .
>
> (2) It is positively useless to persecute the Jew, take away from him his goods, or place him in a ghetto, because he may accept that circumstance and will find a way through it. He will be resurrected when given the chance, because those same ones that are willing to beat him, eventually will protect him. . . .

> (3) When persecuted, humiliated, or molested anywhere on the planet, the Jew will expand his solidarity with other Jews, because precisely in that he finds his dignity. . . . And in that sense, the Jewish character and his diasporic pride will be confirmed when his attachment to other Jews is awakened.[6]

Gerchunoff calls at first for intellectual protests against anti-Semitic acts because he thinks he may persuade his enemy by intellectual means. That persuasion remained a hope, not a reality. As time went on, he sank into disillusionment and silence, and eventually isolated himself from his community.

Although he became quite enthusiastic about certain Jewish topics, such as the Talmud, he remained evasive and ambivalent. When Jewish symbols appear in his late fiction, it is always in a remote and distant context, with reference to Heinrich Heine or Baruch Spinoza, never the current scene. His dream of a Promised Land in South America was slowly collapsing, along with other liberal values. At the outbreak of World War II in 1939, about 218,000 Jews lived in Argentina. Yet only a decade later, the country turned into a nightmare for all integrationist hopes.

Arguably the most horrific events in that nightmare took place in 1994, when the AMIA (Asociación Mutual Israelita Argentina), the Jewish Community Center in Buenos Aires, was the target of a terrorist attack that left almost a hundred people dead and many more injured. The event took place more than two years after another anti-Semitic attack in Buenos Aires, this one against the Israeli Embassy. Twenty-nine people died and more than two hundred were injured.

The investigation to the AMIA attack led to Iran, but the then-president Carlos Saúl Menem, who was of Lebanese descent, impeded a thorough investigation. As a result, the wounds remained open. The AMIA attack was the first major terrorist incident against Jews not only in Argentina but also in Latin America. The outcome of that event left the Jewish communities in the region vulnerable, fearful of further aggressions. While Gerchunoff couldn't have foreseen the atrocities, in his disenchantment he produced a litany that augured a time when Jews would become individualized as objects of animosity.

The incident serves as a bookend to Borges's intellectual quest because politics infringed on Argentine Jewish life in cathartic ways. The detached, cosmopolitan Jew that is ubiquitous in his stories and poems became even more of an anachronism, an ethereal creature only capable of existing as an abstraction. A number of journalistic investigations as well as literary works and movies have been produced around the terrorist attack.

A decade after it, ten directors, including Daniel Burman and Alberto Lecchi, made a film anthology titled after the date of the attack, *18-j* (2004). Also, in 2009 Marcos Carnevale premiered *Anita*, about a young woman with Down Syndrome who wanders Buenos Aires after her mother is killed in the AMIA bombing. Among others, Gustavo D. Perednik published a fictionalized chronicle called *Matar sin que se note* (*Killing without Trace*, 2009). Also, along with Marcelo Brodsky, I created a *fotonovela* about the preparations for the attack called *Once @ 9:53am* (2012).

The history of Jewish Argentine literature includes many others considered to be Gerchunoff's successors. Among them is César Tiempo (pseudonym of Israel Zeitlin, 1906–1980), a famous-in-his-time playwright, critic, and poet, who had emigrated to Argentina from Ukraine. He was highly esteemed as a man of letters and travel writer whose poetry almost uniquely refers to one central metaphor: the Sabbath. This interest is reflected in some of the titles of his works: *Book for the Break of the Sabbath*, published in 1930, or *Joyful Saturday*, which appeared in 1955.

He always willingly wrote for a gentile audience and, probably influenced by Israel Zangwill's *Dreamers of the Ghetto*, used the vivid imagery of the Buenos Aires Jewish ghetto to draw an appealing distinction between the Jewish and Christian Sabbaths. As a liberal, Tiempo identified with the oppressed and humiliated, and favored a multiethnic society. His two famous theatrical pieces, *I Am the Theater* and *Creole Bread*, staged in the thirties, dealt with the subject of assimilation and Jewish versus gentile justice.

Like Gerchunoff, he was deeply depressed by outbursts of anti-Semitism; yet unlike him, he actively responded with written arguments and oral protests against the racist campaign inspired by the infamous writings of the propagandist Gustavo Martínez Zuviría. The director of the National Library in Buenos Aires, Zuviría, under the pen name of Hugo Wast, had written both *The Kahal and Gold* in 1938, inspired by *The Protocols of the Elders of Zion*, the infamous anti-Semitic tract immensely popular, even today, throughout Latin America. Yet despite Tiempo's public complaints, nothing changed. At times, even the national press, as if echoing his own writing, denied the presence of racial tension in the country. As with Gerchunoff, the political events helped develop in him a deeply rooted skepticism about Argentina's democratic future, and they also frightened his young Jewish followers.

Another important Jewish figure in Argentine literature is Bernardo Verbitsky (1907–1979), a prolific realist writer who published long novels dealing with Jewish identity in contemporary Argentina and the world at large. They include *Hard to Start Living* (1941), which is an essential text for understanding the cultural situation of Buenos Aires in the thirties. The critic and novelist David Viñas (1929–2011), whom I mentioned in reference to the *Semana Trágica*, in his novel *Dar la Cara* (1962), argues for a nation that is at once multiethnic, democratic, and tolerant.

Jewish writers and intellectuals of later generations suffered the horrors of military dictatorship, persecution, violence, and exile. Among them was Luisa Mercedes Levinson, half-Jewish and a close friend and colleague of Borges, who wrote "The Cove"; she is the mother of the Argentine-born New York experimentalist Luisa Valenzuela, author of *The Lizard's Tail* (1985).

Another crucial name is Germán Rozenmacher (1936–1971), a talented young man who felt that the constant attempt to participate in the country's everyday life created deep psychological scars among the Jews. The protagonists of his stories, collected in one volume in 1970, are lonely creatures, many of them failed artists with identity problems, who aspire to enter gentile society but are unable to do so. His tenacious belief in assimilation always brings the reader to the conclusion that for him no Jewish existence proud of its accomplishments could flourish in his native Argentina. In "Blues in the Night," Vassily Goloboff, a music professor who once sang in the Moscow Opera and rejected his Jewish name and identity after immigrating to Buenos Aires, returns to religion in his later years. In the tradition of the encounter between Leopold Bloom and Stephen Dedalus, one day he has a sudden rendezvous with Bernardo, a young Jew, in which they share memories about broken families and talk about their enchantment with *I Pagliacci*. But no happiness comes to them in the end.

In the same generation as Rozenmacher are the storyteller Mario Goloboff (b. 1939), the author of a trilogy that includes the 1984 novel *Pigeon Keeper*, about rural life in the mythical town of Algarrobos; Humberto Costantini (1924–1987); Pedro Orgambide (b. 1928); Isidoro Blaisten (1933–2004); Alicia Steimberg (1933–2012); Marcos Aguinis (b. 1935); Ricardo Feierstein (b. 1942); Cecilia Absatz (b. 1943); Aída Bortnik (b. 1943); Nora Glickman (b. 1942); Mario Satz (b. 1944); Marcos Ricardo Barnatán (b. 1946); Mario Szichman (b. 1945); Ana María Shua (b. 1951), Marcelo Birmajer (b. 1966); and Andrés Neuman (b. 1977).

Szichman, the author of *At 8:25 Evita Became Immortal* (1983), is particularly interesting. In the late 1960s he tried to create a family saga that would encapsulate the diverse personalities and viewpoints among Argentine Jews and explore relevant issues such as the community's response to Israel, assimilation, the world of business, and religion. It is quite obvious that not only the works of Gabriel García Márquez, but also Yiddish novels such as I. J. Singer's *The Family Carnovsky* (1988), made a transforming impression on him. He shows some of the stylistic elements of magical realism—a narrative style made popular after the publication of *One Hundred Years of Solitude* (1967), which mixes reality with dreamlike components and uses as its setting the exotic Latin American landscape—but he is more concerned with genealogy and tradition within the family circle. In *The Jews of Mar Dulce* (1971), *The False Chronicle* (1969, revised in 1972), and *At 8:25 Evita Became Immortal*, the Pechof family is followed from their immigration in 1918, their rejection of gaucho agricultural life, and their transition to the urban life of Buenos Aires during the thirties and forties.

Although the narrative moves back and forth in time, Szichman stops around 1952, when his characters discover their unacceptable status as Jews in Argentina and desperately struggle to assimilate by changing their surname to Gutiérrez Anselmi. By means of an ironic, self-hating point of view, mixing Yiddishisms with a convoluted Spanish, the author builds a vision of the impossibility of Diaspora life in Argentina as he recreates the customs and idiosyncrasies of Jewish life in South America with astonishing detail. Unlike Gerchunoff, Berele or Bernardo (Szichman's alter ego) is permanently searching for an answer to his father's strange, political death in the city dump. And by deciphering his father's last intentions, Berele discovers the cause of the entire family's dilemma.

What is interesting about Szichman's fiction is the way it revises national history. By placing his characters in a variety of periods, from the *Semana Trágica* to the military coups in the forties and the defeated revolution in 1956 (when Berele's father perishes), Szichman makes an unquestionable statement:

no regime, no juncture, in Argentine history is good for the Jews because their historical presence on the River Plate is a mistake.

If Gerchunoff at one time believed Argentina to be a heaven, Szichman sees it as hell.

Borges, in contrast, perceived it (and most everything else) as both. As a young man, he traveled with his family to Europe, where they were caught up by World War I. Five years later, they all returned to Buenos Aires. The contrast between the Old World and the New affected him deeply. His return home exposed him to a series of national types (e.g., gauchos, *compadritos*, and *orilleros*) that, in his eyes, summed up Argentina's character. As with religion, he developed a purely intellectual attraction toward them. What is startling is the way in which he achieved universality by focusing on these sets of native types. Not only did he write sonnets about his military ancestors, but from his first short story, "Streetcorner Man," on to his volume of tales, *The Book of Sand* (1975), Argentina's historical characters and its folklore figure prominently in his work.

Years later, with his friend and collaborator Adolfo Bioy Casares, he edited a two-volume anthology of *gaucho* literature. And he produced brilliant essays on subjects like the Argentinean language and on local men of letters such as Evaristo Carriego, Paul Groussac, and Leopoldo Lugones. Borges, as one of his biographers, James Woodall, stated, "was steeped in the poetry of his Argentine predecessors, *gaucho* traditions and *porteño* slang, as he was in the stories of Henry James and the novels of Franz Kafka."

A story by Borges emblematic of his relationship with Jews in Argentina is "Unworthy," included in *Doctor Brodie's Report* (1970). As its title suggests, the theme returns to the issue of unworthiness at the heart of Borges's oeuvre. Architecturally, it is shaped as a story within a story. The introductory part has Borges describe his friendship with a Jewish businessman, don Santiago Fischbein, the owner of the Librería Buenos Aires, on Calle Talcahuano. By the time the narrative begins Fischbein has died. This allows Borges to release the information free of guilt. This early section allows for insightful views on politics in Argentina:

> Fischbein had tended toward the obese; his features are not as clear in my memory as our long conversations are. Firmly yet coolly he would condemn Zionism—it would make the Jew an ordinary man, he said, tied like all other men to a single tradition and a single country, and bereft of the complexities and discords that now enrich him. I recall that he once told me that a new edition of the works of Baruch Spinoza was being prepared, which would banish all that Euclidean apparatus that makes Spinoza's work so difficult to read yet at the same time imparts an illusory sense of rigor to the fantastic theory. Fischbein showed me (though he refused to sell me) a curious copy of Rosenroth's *Kabbala Denudata*, but my library does contain some books by Ginsburg and Waite that bear Fischbein's seal.

Fischbein himself then takes control of the narrative. He recounts to Borges an anecdote of his past that defined him. The anecdote is about Fischbein's youth, when he was still struggling as a Jew to become Argentinean. "I don't know whether I've ever mentioned that I'm from Entre Ríos," he states. "I won't tell you that we were Jewish gauchos—there were never any Jewish gauchos. We were merchants and small farmers." In a single, decisive stroke, Borges demystifies the tradition of Jewish gauchos eulogized by Gerchunoff and others. Kindling a debate that continues to this day, he suggests that the early chapter of the

Ashkenazi immigration to Argentina, turned through nostalgia into a usable bucolic past, is fiction.

The sociological component in story becomes even more tangible, as does the debate on identity. How have Argentine Jews solved their dilemma of belonging? How do they understand the concept of homeland? Fischbein's parents moved to family to Buenos Aires, where they opened a store. They lived in a neighborhood where there were streetcorner gangs. The anecdote Fischbein tells is of his friendship to one of them, a *compadrito* whom he perceived as a hero: Francisco Ferrari. "He had black hair and was rather tall, good-looking—handsome in the style of those days. He always wore black." Soon Fischbein engages in an intimidating encounter with Ferrari. In one, a gang harasses him and Ferrari rescues him. Fischbein idealizes him and Ferrari invites him to his clan. It happens, again, just as Fischbein is struggling to find his Jewish Argentine identity. "I don't know how to explain it to you," Fischbein tells Borges:

> Today I've carved out a place for myself. I have this bookstore that I enjoy and whose books I read; I have friendships, like ours; I have my wife and children; I've joined the Socialist party—I'm a good Argentine and a good Jew. I am respected and respectable. The man you see now is almost bald; at the time I was a poor Jewish kid with red hair in a tough neighborhood on the outskirts of the city. People looked askance at me. I tried, as all young fellows do, to be like everyone else. I had started calling myself Santiago to make the Jacob go away, but there was nothing I could do about the Fischbein. We all come to resemble the image others have of us: I sensed people's contempt for me, and I felt contempt for myself as well. At that time, and especially in that setting, it was important to be brave; I knew myself to be a coward. Women

> intimidated me; deep down, I was ashamed of my fainthearted chastity. I had no friends my own age.

At that precise moment, Ferrari invites Fischbein to be part of a robbery. He includes him in the planning stages and gives him a specific role. Fischbein's self-esteem improves temporarily:

> Friendship, you know, is as mysterious as love or any other state of this confusion we call life. In fact, I have sometimes suspected that the only thing that holds no mystery is happiness, because it is its own justification. However that may be, the fact was that Francisco Ferrari, the daring, strong Ferrari, felt a sense of friendship for me, contemptible me. I felt he was mistaken, that I was not worthy of that friendship. I tried to avoid him, but he wouldn't let me. My anxiety was made worse by my mother's disapproval; she could not resign herself to my associating with what she called "the riffraff," nor to the fact that I'd begun to ape them.[7]

True to his unworthiness, Fischbein becomes an informer—a Jewish informer. Shortly before the robbery, he goes to the police station and lets the authorities—the hated authorities—in on the details of the plot. One of the officers asks him: "Are you making the accusations because you think you're a good citizen? Is that it?" The response is symptomatic: "I didn't feel he'd understand, so I answered. 'Yes, sir. I'm a good Argentine.'"

As expected, in the middle of the robbery the police appear. Fischbein hears four shots. Ferrari's body and that of one of his accomplices is dragged out of the building. They had been short at point-blank range. Fischbein adds: "In their report the police said the robbers had failed to halt when they were ordered, and that Ferrari and don Eliseo had fired the first shots. I knew that was a lie, because I had never seen either of them with a revolver. The police had taken advantage of the occasion to settle an old score."

In other words, Borges explores the challenges of nationality not through simplification. Jews might not have been gauchos, but they are everything else: lawyers, doctors, thieves, prostitutes. "Unworthy" is a story of guilt and betrayal. A pseudo-Jewish Gaucho enters the word of gangs and hopes to become a *compadrito*. But in the end he is incapable of establishing his bonds to that world and joins ranks with the wrong side: the police.

Borges frames the narrative from the perspective of Jewish belonging. Are Jews Argentines? Superficially they are, sometime in spite of themselves. But as perennial outsiders, they will never truly penetrate the Argentine psyche. In other words, they might be Argentines on paper, but they'll never be *compadritos*. Even though it might appear to be, this is not an indictment by Borges. Instead, it is a celebration. Borges was envious of *compadritos*. They were courageous. They were brave. He instead was simply an intellectual attempting to understand what the Argentine tradition is about. Fischbein, then, is just like Borges: an interloper, a falsifier, more connected with books than with life itself.

~

I once dreamed of putting together a volume of Borgeana about Jews. It would include "Unworthy" as well as a myriad essays and poems I intend to mention in this series. At the center of it would be my own favorite Borges stories, including "*Deutsches Requiem*" and "Emma Zunz," the two dealing with Ashkenazi Jews. "Emma Zunz," included in *The Aleph* (1949), might well be his best, although it is also among his strangest, for no other reason than the fact that Borges seldom features a female protagonist in his oeuvre, let alone a rebellious one, taking the law in her own hands, as this one does. I wrote about it years ago from the perspective of Jewish theodicy: characters that defy social rules and compete with the divine.

The story takes place in early 1922, as the female protagonist, Emma Zunz, receives a letter from Brazil announcing the death of her father, Manuel Meier, also known as Emanuel Zunz. Although she is told he died of an accidental overdose of Veronal (that is, a suicide), she knows better. She recalls a scandal in his business and the fact that her father's partner, Aaron Loewenthal, drove him to his end. Borges devotes himself to exploring Emma's inner emotions and her determination to take revenge. Indeed, this is a story of an individual taking the law into her own hands.

Emma recognizes that, since the facts about Loewenthal aren't known, human law is unlikely to put him on trial. Her option, then, is to devise a stratagem in order to make Loewenthal pay for his crime but in such way that Emma is not deemed a criminal. "She did not sleep that night, and by the time first light defined the rectangle of the window, she had perfected her plan. In the mill, there were rumors of a strike; Emma declared, as she always did, that she was opposed to all forms of violence."

What is Emma's plan? She's still a virgin. She decides to go to the pier and have herself deflowered by an anonymous Scandinavian sailor. She then goes to Aaron Loewenthal's office above the mill when he's alone. She pretends to have been sexually abused by him and then kills him with a revolver. The actual scene of revenge is described in a complex manner. Herein the English translation by Andrew Hurley that is part of the volume *Collected Fictions* (1998):

> Sitting before Aaron Loewenthal, Emma felt (more than the urgency to avenge her father) the urgency to punish the outrage she herself had suffered. She could not *not* kill him, after being so fully and thoroughly dishonored. Nor did she have time to waste

> in theatrics. Sitting timidly in his office, she begged Loewenthal's pardon, invoked (in her guise as snitch) the obligations entailed by loyalty, mentioned a few names, insinuated others, and stopped short, as through overcome by fearfulness. Her performance succeeded; Loewenthal went out to get her a glass of water. By the time he returned from the dining hall, incredulous at the woman's fluttering perturbation yet full of solicitude, Emma had found the heavy revolver in the drawer. She pulled the trigger twice. Loewethanl's considerable body crumpled as though crushed by the explosions and the smoke; the glass of water shattered; his face looked at her with astonishment and fury; the mouth in the face cursed her in Spanish and Yiddish.

Borges's scene is strikingly cinematic. He focuses on the gun, then on the victim. He then allows Emma a few dramatic words: "I have avenged by father, and I shall not be punished . . ." "Emma Zunz" concludes in a philosophical tone:

> Then she picked up the telephone and repeated what she was to repeat so many times, in those and other words: Something has happened, something unbelievable . . . Sr. Loewethnal sent for me on the pretext of the strike . . . He raped me . . . I killed him . . .
>
> The story was unbelievable, yes—and yet it convinced everyone, because in substance it was true. Emma Zunz's tone of voice was real, her shame was real, her hatred was real. The outrage that had been done to her was real, as well; all that was false were the circumstances, the time, and one or two proper names.

It's important to focus on the rape scene—the only such description ever included by Borges in his fiction. When Emma goes to the pier, her approach is mimetic. She enters a few bars in order to study the way women behave toward men in such places. She then looks for a possible suitor. Having identified a young one, she fears he might inspire in her tenderness. She opts for another "so that there might be no mitigation of the purity of the horror." The sailor (a Swede or Finn) takes her down a hallway which leads outside. He did not speak Spanish. "He was an instrument for Emma," Borges writes, "as she was for him—but she was use for pleasure, while he was used for justice."

> When she was alone, Emma did not open her eyes immediately. On the night table was the money the man had left. Emma sat up and tore it to shreds, as she had torn up the letter a short time before. Tearing up money is an act of impiety, like throwing away bread; the minute she did it, Emma wished she hadn't—an act of pride and on *that* day. . . . Foreboding melted into the sadness of her body, into the revulsion. Sadness and revulsion lay upon Emma like chains, but slowly she got up and began to dress.[8]

Like in a black and white Hollywood film, the carnal encounter isn't as much described as it is insinuated. Why doesn't Borges detail the actual moment of horror? Instead, he concentrates on Emma's mental—and spiritual—plight: what she experiences after the act has been consummated.

Why does Borges set the plot amidst Yiddish-speaking immigrants? As a result of his financial dealings, her father has been forced to run to southern Brazil, specifically to the Rio Grande do Sul province. He has also changed his identity by opting for another name. Emma's memory brings her back to her childhood in the province of Entre Ríos. But she lives in Calle Liniers, in Lanús, a middle-class neighborhood in southwestern Buenos Aires. Aaron Loewenthal's mill is on Warnes Street, in central Buenos Aires, near the Villa Crespo commercial district.

Do the names of these immigrants signal a connection to the world of the *shtetl*? Emma is the daughter of a newcomer, an Argentine by birth. Thus, she is a full citizen. But she still acts like an outsider. Rather than trusting the judicial system, she resorts to implementing her own punishment against her father's victimizer. Some critics approach the text from a psychoanalytic perspective: Emma and her father are united by a natural pact, which she sanctifies when an outsider disturbs their union. Other scholars have struggled to understand the story from an esoteric perspective. They approach Emma Zunz as the kabbalistic myth of the *Shekhinah*, the female part of God. Aizenberg states in *The Aleph Weaver* (1984):

> Emma, her wronged and exiled father, and the embezzler, Aaron Loewenthal, reenact the mystical story of God's Daughter—the feminine hypostasis of the divine—who is separated from her heavenly progenitor and falls into an unclean physical-sexual world as a result of sin. Since the Daughter is God the Father's power of stern judgment, she proceeds to punish the wrong-doer through destruction and violence, without, however, restoring the harmony which existed in the happy days before the sin.[9]

I believe that Borges, who was still in his forties when he crafted "Emma Zunz" (it originally appeared in the prestigious intellectual magazine *Sur* 167, September 1948), made Emma's odyssey far more mundane. The plot was given to him by his friend Cecilia Ingenieros. Borges in turn dedicated the story to her, as rather, "I was not so much dedicating it to her as giving it to her back." The names of his characters—as is typical—aren't accidental. The words Emma and *Zunz* are made of four letters each, like the Tetragramathon, that is, the divine name. The repetition of the letters m and z in them accentuates this relation. In an interview, Borges said: "I was trying to get an ugly and at the same time a colorless name. . . . [T]he name seems so meaningless, so insignificant."

If Borges was conscious at all, Zunz, Meir, and Loewenthal have a Germanic extraction. This suggests that Borges places his story in the context of educated Yiddish speakers from the Rhim whose view of their Polish and Ukrainian counterparts was unfavorable. They perceived themselves as cosmopolitan, whereas the *shtetl* people were ignoramuses. Seen through this prism, the characters might have yet another element of discomfort toward Argentine society: they are upper-class snobs, unrelated to the proletarian Tevyes and Yentls whose manners are stereotypes by gentile society. In other words, they are at home neither among Jews nor among non-Jews.

Still, the question persists: Why does Borges make Emma Zunz a Jew? It isn't clear from interviews if Cecilia Ingenieros offered him the story with the Jewish ingredients already set. Most likely, Borges inserted them as he crafted the final outcome. Even though he makes Emma a nonobservant Jew, her religious ancestry emphasizes the rebellious spirit he wants to infuse in her. The female protagonist is Jewish because Borges designs his tale in the interstices between divine and human law. Emma is aware of Loewenthal's crime but knows no human court will convict him.

What choice does she have? She isn't a believer, which means she cannot abate her sense of justice: she won't be calmed by the thought that Loewenthal will be punished in the afterlife. Solution: to plot her own punishment. This places her in the tradition of biblical characters: if society isn't ready to hand out a sentence, she is ready to do it herself. Borges's Jewishness emphasizes individual responsibility above social conventions. It also stresses spiritual purity above all. But it stresses a connection between the heavenly and earthly domains. Emma's decision to give up her virginity so as to avenge her father is a sign that the higher order is more important than integrity. She is ready to sacrifice herself for an abstract idea of justice.

"Emma Zunz," finally, is also about stereotypes. Manuel Meier and Aaron Loewenthal are businessmen. Money is in their mind. Money becomes a source of dispute. They speak Yiddish. One kills the other. This is the pecuniary world of Shakespeare's Shylock. But Emma's action unsettles the stereotypes: she sacrifices herself in order to achieve a superior form of justice. She is also a feminist figure eager to prove that women aren't passive. Why call her *Emma*? Easy: as a tribute to Emma Bovary and Emma Woodhouse, strong-willed women in the Western canon who refuse to conform to the male establishment.

Talking about stereotypes, which, striving from Platonic figures, condense the various aspects of an item into a unified, if falsified, entity, in 1977 Borges delivered seven lectures on seven different topics in seven nights in Buenos Aires. The topics he chose included nightmares, *The Divine Comedy*, poetry, *The Arabian Nights*, Buddhism, and the Kabbalah. The transcripts of the lectures were published in book form in 1980 as *Seven Nights*. Marvelous as these disquisitions are in their encyclopedic broadness, Borges also reduces his themes to a series of similes. Arguably the most inspiring of the lectures was the last one, on blindness.

Of course, Borges, since early childhood, knew he would one day become blind. It was congenital in his illness. His father, among other relatives, was also blind. And blindness struck librarians in Argentina who, like him, were directors of the National Library, Paul José Marmol and Groussac. What is inspiring about Borges's lecture is the resignation with which he approaches his argument. He talks of different blind writers: Homer, John Milton, W. H. Prescott (the historian who wrote *Conquest of Mexico* and *Conquest of Peru*), and Joyce. Borges states (in Eliot Weinberger's translation):

> People generally imagine the blind as enclosed in a black world. There is, for example, Shakespeare's line: "Looking into darkness which the blind don't

> see." If we understand "darkness" as "blackness," then Shakespeare is wrong.

Borges adds that the blind live in a universe that is inconvenient, but no more so than any other inconvenience that affects those people able to see. And herein his message, in which he uses misfortune as a way to appreciate life. This appreciation comes from his love for Jews, who have turned suffering into vision:

> A writer lives. The task of being a poet is not completed at a fixed schedule. No one is a poet from eight to twelve and from two to six. Whoever is a poet is always one, and continually assaulted by poetry. I suppose a painter feels that colors and shapes are besieging him. Or a musician feels the strange world of sounds—the strangest world of art—is always seeking him out, that there are melodies and dissonances looking for him. For the task of an artist, blindness is not a total misfortune. It may be an instrument. Fray Luis de León dedicated one of his most beautiful odes to Francisco Salinas, a blind musician.
>
> A writer, or any man, must believe that whatever happens to him is an instrument; everything has been given for an end. This is even stronger in the case of the artist. Everything that happens, including humiliations, embarrassments, misfortunes, all has been given like clay, like material for one's art. One must accept it.[10]

PART II

DEUTSCHES REQUIEM

Who shall tell me if you, Israel, are to be found in the lost labyrinth of the secular rivers that is my blood?

—"To Israel" (1969)

The consensus among Borges's biographers and critics is that he was deeply apolitical and that, throughout his life, he remained disengaged with, even apathetic to, local, national, and international affairs. There is some truth to this position, but taking it at face value runs the risk of oversimplifying his position. It is true that Borges was, especially in his adolescence, a dilettante à la Oscar Wilde minus the ornamental outspokenness. But he invariably managed to volunteer political comments on current events, even if these comments were saturated with sarcasm and parody, which at times made them appear to be the remarks of an amateur. And yet, they were quite forceful, not to say acerbic.

For instance, Borges denounced Hitler almost from the start, decrying the arrival of Nazism as a catastrophe for German culture. A partial yet enlightening record of his opinions is to be found *Selected Non-Fictions*, edited by Eliot Weinberger. It includes a full section devoted to the years 1937–1945. Many of the pieces in it are well known to English-language readers, but a handful are not; and a few among them are thereby translated by the first time.

Of the entire bunch, only a small portion address the events in Europe; still, they are significant in that they allow a glimpse of Borges's beliefs and the trenchant style with which he debunked nasty stereotypes. In one, "A Pedagogy of Hatred," he attacks the publication, in Germany of the children's book *Trau keinem Fuchs auf grüner Heid und keinem Jud bei seinem Eid* [Don't Trust Any Fox from a Heath or Any Jew on his Oath], which, according to the Argentine, "has already sold 51,000 copies." He adds: "Displays of hatred are even more obscure and denigrating than exhibitions," then proceeds to dissect the anti-Semitic volume. Herein the translation by Suzanne Jill Levine included in Weinberger's *Selected Non-Fictions*:

> Take any page: for example, page 5. Here I find, not without justifiable bewilderment, this didactic poem—"The German is a proud man who knows how to work and struggle. Jews detest him because he is so handsome and enterprising"—followed by an equally informative and explicit quatrain: "Here's a Jew, recognizable to all, the biggest scoundrel in the whole kingdom. He thinks he's wonderful, and he's horrible." The engravings are more astute: the German is a Scandinavian, eighteen-year-old athlete, plainly portrayed as a worker; the Jew is a dark Turk, obese and middle-aged. Another sophistic feature is that the German is clean-shaven and the Jew, while bald, is very hairy. (It is well known that German Jews are *Ashkenazim*, copper-haired Slavs. In this book they are presented as dark half-breeds so that they'll appear to be the exact opposite of the blond beasts. Their attributes also include the permanent use of a fez, a rolled cigar, and ruby rings.)[1]

Borges ends his exposition as follows: "What can one say about such a book? Personally, I am outraged, less for Israel's sake than for Germany's, less for the offended community than for the offensive nation."

The list of Borges's anti-Nazi nonfiction rejoinders includes another piece, this one drafted in 1938, in which he complains of the fact that in a revised edition done by Johannes Rohr to *Geschichte der deutschen National-Literatur*, by A. F. C. Vilmar, a number of entries on Goethe, Lessing, and Nietzsche have been mutilated, and the catalogue that includes seven hundred authors, "incredibly, silences the name of Heine." The Argentine was an unequivocal admirer of German literature and was in distress by its decline. "I don't know if the world can do without German civilization," he wrote in the highbrow magazine *Sur*, edited by his loyal friend and admirer Victoria Ocampo; and, in another issue of the same journal, he stated: "It is unarguable that a [German] victory would see the ruin and debasement of the world."

This type of erudite judgment only had a limited impact on public opinion. Still, Borges, perhaps because no other channel fitted him well, regularly used the word—printed, oral—to denounce the excesses of fascism. And yet, the outside world succeeded in reminding him that Germanophilia was on the rise in Argentina. In 1939, a small incident, narrated without consequence by some biographers, brought the war closer to home, though. In Punte del Este, Uruguay, the British attempted to sink the *Graf Spee*, a German battleship. The ship took refuge in Montevideo but was expelled by the Uruguayan government, at the time in support of the Allies. The British fleet awaited the ship, which the German crew itself eventually sank, and the Germans escaped to Argentina.

This result was discouraging, but to Borges and others it only confirmed the country's endorsement of Nazism. This openness to receive refugees from Germany would continue until after World War II, when former officers and soldiers, with fake passports, were allowed entrance and protection, at times making a life in the same neighborhoods where survivors of concentration camps and other Jewish refugees moved. Probably the most famous of these was Adolf Eichmann, whose case because a *cause célèbre* when, after he had been located by the Nazi hunter Simon Wiesenthal, Mossad, the Israeli Secret Service, in a thunderbolt rescue operation, flew him out of Argentina and into Israel before the news of his capture was made public worldwide.

Finally, in an essay of 1940 that is probably the most important one—surely the most discussed—by the Argentine on the topic, called "Definition of a Germanophile," Borges openly ridiculed "Germanophiles" [*germanófilos*] in his country. He portrayed them as monstrous people whose knowledge of German civilization was sketchy at best and who indulged in recognizable acts of censorship of the most egregious form of their own culture, often verging on Anglophobia as they foolishly described the excesses of the English people in Europe. These Germanophiles, Borges stated, were nothing but admirers of Hitler, "not in spite of the high-altitude bombs and the rumbling invasions, the machine guns, the accusations and lies, but because of those acts and instruments." He then added:

> He is delighted by evil and atrocity. The triumph of Germany does not matter to him; he wants the humiliation of England and a satisfying burning of London. He admires Hitler as he once admired his precursors in the criminal underworld of Chicago. The discussion becomes impossible because of the offenses I ascribe to Hitler are, for him, wonders and virtues. . . . The Hitlerist is always a spiteful man, and a secret and sometimes public worshiper of criminal "vivacity" and cruelty. He is, thanks to a poverty of imagination, a man who believes that the

> future cannot be different from the present, and that Germany, till now victorious, cannot lose. He is the cunning man who longs to be on the winning side."[2]

By the time the war ended, Borges was forty-six. He greeted the news of the liberation of Paris with a sense of inexhaustible exhilaration. That exhilaration he articulated in full in an essay that has been insufficiently read, and even less studied in detail: "A Comment on August 23, 1944." In it Borges discusses the multiple contradictions of the many Argentineans that supported Nazism. He lists their contradictions, which he prefers to call "incoherences."

I hereby list a handful: they adore the German race, but they abhor "Saxon" America; they condemn the articles of Versailles, but they applaud the wonders of the *Blitzkrieg*; they are anti-Semitic, but they profess a religion of Hebrew origin; and they idolize San Martín, but they regard the independence of America as a mistake. The last paragraph of the essay reverberates in Borges's fiction, as I will show later on in these pages:

> For Europeans and Americans, one order and only one is possible; it used to be called Rome, and now it is called Western Culture. To be a Nazi (to play the energetic barbarian, Viking, Tartar, sixteenth-century conquistador, gaucho, or Indian) is, after all, mentally and morally impossible. Nazism suffers from unreality, like [John Scotus] Erigena's hell. It is uninhabitable; men can only die for it, lie for it, wound or kill for it. No one, in the intimate depths of his being, can wish it to triumph. I shall risk this conjecture: *Hitler wants to be defeated.* Hitler is blindly collaborating with the inevitable armies that will annihilate him, as the metal vultures and the dragon (which must have known that they were monsters) collaborated, mysteriously, with Hercules.[3]

The sentence, italicized by Borges himself, is, in my eyes, a paradigm: Hitler wanted to succeed in his campaign to dominate the planet, the Argentine argues, yet, upon realizing that the endeavor was impossible, he deliberately sought to be crushed, that is, he indulged in an effort that could only culminate in his own defeat. For this defeat Hitler saw as a triumph: a triumph of evil over good, a triumph of barbarism over civilization.

The paradigm is best articulated in another aspect of Borges's response to Nazism: his fiction. I shall now devote my attention to it, but not before offering a handful of comments that should serve as counterpoint to the inventory of quotes and reflections I've submitted so far. While in his nonfiction the Argentine regularly discussed the impact of fascism at home, in his stories he took a different route: every tale on the subject is set in Europe, from Czechoslovakia to Germany itself. Why is this so?

Maybe it was because it allowed Borges to tackle the issue frontally, to go to the source; and because he knew well that, since these pieces were in Spanish, their immediate impact would take place in Argentina. Another significant feature is that none of these fictions takes place inside a concentration camp, nor do they make reference to gas chambers or any other method of extermination. And yet, they tackle the Holocaust fearlessly, in a fashion far more overt that almost anything produced by Argentine literati in those decades.

~

"*Deutsches Requiem*," about which I have more to say, is also, curiously, about faith, endurance, and posterity—but of a different sort. As fiction it is flawed, yet it contains the seed of a more mature, developed viewpoint by Borges than the majority of the nonfiction pieces about the war that I listed above. He drafted it a bit later than "The Secret Miracle," and it was collected in his subsequent collection of stories *The Aleph* (1949). Otto Dietrich zur Linde, the narrator, is a former German officer who in his youth was an avid reader of Schopenhauer and a listener of Brahms but who, somehow, cohered to the Nazi party, advancing in rank in 1941 to become subdirector of the Tarnowitz concentration camp. Zur Linde, from his cell, offers a diatribe about the battle for Nazi supremacy of the globe and, thus, delivers a justification for Hitler's actions. Borges uses the character as a springboard to explore the psyche of a "Germanophile."

Toward the last third of the story, though, zur Linde comes across a camp inmate who changes forever his views: the famous poet David Jerusalem. Is it emblematic that neither of these characters, zur Linde and Jerusalem—nor Hladik, for that matter—were real-life individuals? By all means: Borges prefers to work on composites, seeking to define archetypal figures that represent not one single person but humanity as a whole. This quality of unreality is, in fact, what the Argentine is after: a sense that people are not as different from one another as they might believe themselves to be; instead, that they are version, or at best variations, of a Platonic ideal. The following lines, in a footnote by an anonymous editor in "*Deutsches Requiem*" (it is Borges himself, of course), ratify this assumption:

> In neither the files nor the published work of Sögel does Jerusalem's name appear. Nor does one find it in the histories of German literature. I do not, however, think that this is an invented figure. Many Jewish intellectuals were tortured in Tarnowitz on the orders of Otto Dietrich zur Linde, among them the pianist Emma Rosenzweig. "David Jerusalem" is perhaps a symbol for many individuals. We are told that he died on March 1, 1943; on March 1, 1939, the narrator had been wounded at Tilsit. [Ed.][4]

In any event, the protagonist says of Jerusalem that he was "the prototypical Sephardic Jew, although he belonged to the depraved and hated Ashkenazim." Zur Linde becomes obsessed with his victim: the talent of his hexameters, the capacity to consecrate his genius to hymns of happiness. His obsession and his admiration accentuate his repulsion. In due time, he drives Jerusalem insane, and forces him to commit suicide. By killing Jerusalem, zur Linde trusts that he will able to eradicate his own compassion.

But sooner rather than later he realizes that what we must detest in the outer world has a chamber in our own soul; that those we hold as victims are actually an essential part of ourselves. It is here that the italicized sentence from Borges's above-mentioned essay "A Comment on August 23, 1944" acquires its full meaning. *Hitler wants to be defeated*: as the Nazi ponders his own destiny, he acknowledges that everywhere in the universe evil is the reverse of good and, therefore, Nazism and Judaism are two sides of the same coin. He also admits that Hitler not only brought about but also wanted, his own ruin. Worse even, he announces that the Führer did not fight for the German nation only but for all nations—since every man is all men, each of us simultaneously beautiful and abominable.

It is an attractive idea, which, unfortunately, history often corroborates. Hitler's demise, for instance, coincided, on the national front, with the ascent to power of Juan Domingo Perón, another brutal dictator, one with deceitful socialist aspirations; thus, the era of *Peronismo* begun, and in it Borges once again was, willy-nilly, an active participant. Perón emulated Mussolini and other European tyrants by instigating rowdy youthful groups and by channeling their impetus against Jewish targets, from student groups to full-fledged institutions. During the first of his two regimes, between 1943 and 1945, a series of anti-Semitic events orchestrated by the *Alianza Libertadora Nacionalista* took place, in Buenos Aires in particular.

The endorsement of Nazi values by Perón and his followers was disturbing to Borges, by then a celebrity among a small but solid intellectual elite, as well as among a few fans in France. In a series of declarations, he showed signs of deep concern: "The situation in Argentina," he said, "is very serious, so serious that a great number of Argentines are becoming Nazis without being aware of it. Tempted by promises of social reform—in a society that undoubtedly needs a better organization than the one it now has—many people are letting themselves be seduced by an outsize wave of hatred that is sweeping the country. It is a terrible thing, similar to what happened at the beginning of fascism and Nazism [in Europe]." It was during this period that Borges not only suffered public affront, as one *peronista* after another attacked or ridiculed him; he also was the target of personal humiliation. His mother and sister were arrested and put in prison for a brief period of time, and he himself was demoted from librarian at the Miguel Cané Public Library to the job of inspector of poultry and rabbits in the municipal market of Calle Córdoba, a gesture by the tyrant's entourage indicating the kind of respect that they believed a figure such as Borges truly deserved.

Borges's reaction, in return, was, as expected, nothing short of dignified: he never lost his posture as he pursued in his desire to transform the affront, though metaphor, into a lucid assemblage of essays and stories. Among them was a collaboration with his friend Adolfo Bioy Casares under the pseudonym of H. Bustos Domecq, called "*Monsterfest*" (*La fiesta del monstruo*), published in 1955. A handful of Perón's supporters saw their idol equated to Hitler and, at a time of international remorse about the excesses of Nazism, were offended by it. But they were more offended by the man of letters himself, who, in their view, refused to recognize Perón as the carrier of *una nueva Argentina*. None of this deterred Borges in his quest to unveil the brutal side of the nation's populist leader, nor did it diminish his love for one group of Perón's whipping boys: the Jews.

In a conversation of 1978, Borges, by then old and blind, stated (and I translate): "The preeminence of the Jewish in Western Civilization has to do with the fact that a Jew, aside from being English, French, German or whatever, is always a

Jew. He is not tied by any form of loyalty or especial tradition, which allows him to innovate in science and the arts. In that sense, to be an Argentinan offers an advantage similar to that of the Jew." By this he meant that Argentines might be Hispanic Americans but also, and more emphatically, citizens of the world, and that that division if not stimulating, at least shows the tension between the particular and the universal. To which he added the following in a conversation with Antonio Carrizo four years later: "There are some people that see the Jew as a problem. I see in him a solution."

This view was manifested, as an esthetic doctrine, in the lecture Borges delivered in Buenos Aires that I made reference to in the prologue, "The Argentine Writer and Tradition." In part, he was responding to T. S. Eliot's views expressed in his 1919 piece "Tradition and the Individual Talent." But there was much more, including Borges's intention to revamp Argentine letters from the bottom up. In the lecture he described the local writer in derogatory terms. He said: "The native Argentine, in my understanding, is sardonic, suspicious, over and above everything without illusions, and so utterly lacking in verbal grandiosity that in few can it be forgiven and in none extolled."

Borges wondered what themes the Argentine writer should address. He answered by discussing a tangential argument in Edward Gibbon's *The Decline and Fall of the Roman Empire*, in which Gibbon suggests that "in the Arabian book *par excellence*, in the Koran, there are no camels." Borges argues:

> I believe if there were any doubt as to the authenticity of the Koran, this absence of camels would be sufficient to prove it is an Arabian work. It was written by Mohammed, and Mohammed, as an Arab, had no reason to know that camels were especially Arabian; for him they were a part of reality, he had no reason to emphasize them; on the other hand, the first thing a falsifier, a tourist, an Arab nationalist would do is

> have a surfeit of camel, caravans of camels, on every page; but Mohammed, as an Arab, was unconcerned: he knew he could be an Arab without camels. I think we Argentines can emulate Mohammed, can believe in the possibility of being Argentine without abounding in local color.

Borges wished to see his own role in the world beyond the ghettoized confines of regionalism. By the way, it is the exact same feeling he projected toward the English language: it wasn't his fully, but he would do anything possible to appropriate it. And indeed, his fiction is filled with local types, although their presence is sheer artifice. He turned these local types into a Platonic archetype. And therein his most enduring contribution: he showed that in Latin America, all of us are Xerox copies of a European original, yet in a relativistic world where nothing feels authentic anymore, a Xerox is equally, if not more, valuable.

The Buenos Aires lecture includes a bonus:

> What is Argentine tradition? I believe that this question poses no problem and can easily be solved. I believe that our tradition is the whole of Western culture, and I also believe that we have a right to this tradition, a greater right than that which the inhabitants of one Western nation or another may have. Here I remember an essay by Thorstein Veblen, the North American sociologist, on the intellectual preeminence of Jews in Western culture. He wonders if this preeminence authorizes us to posit an innate Jewish superiority and answers that it does not; he says that Jews are prominent in Western culture because they act within that culture and at the same time do not feel bound to it by any special devotion; therefore, he says, it will always be easier for a Jew than for a non-Jew to make innovations in Western culture.[5]

In admiring the Jew as a wandering type, Borges sought to promote the type of literature that was unconfined by borders, a literature beyond patriotism—universal, belonging to everyone. That universality, in his eyes, was Jewish. What he strove for, as the Xeroxed Jew that he was, was to make the patrimony of the Argentine writer not a little piece of land near the South Pole but the globe entire. And, through his effort, he wanted to be within that culture and at the same time not to feel bound to it. Toward the end of the lecture, he asked his fellow Argentine writers to be bold, innovative, and free, just as Jews in Western culture were. "We should essay all themes, and we cannot limit ourselves to purely Argentine subjects in order to be Argentine; for either being Argentine is an inescapable act of fate—and in that case we shall be so in all events—or being Argentine is a mere affectation, a mask."

PART III

A CATALOG OF JEWISH SYMBOLS

> I detest Hitler precisely because he does not share my faith in the German people.
>
> —"An Essay on Neutrality" (1939)

I have said that Borges was a *rara avis*. The intelligentsia in Latin America, particularly the left-leaning one, has never been particularly interested in things Jewish. It isn't overtly anti-Semitic either, although since the Israeli invasion of Lebanon in 1982 that intelligentsia has become openly anti-Zionist. The line between anti-Semitism and anti-Zionism, in Latin America and elsewhere, is thin to the degree of invisibility.

At any rate, more often than not Jews and their contribution to Western civilization are ignored. Is this silence a form of attack? For instance, in his magisterial oeuvre, Octavio Paz (1914–1996), the Nobel Prize winner in 1990, never once addressed Jewishness in an upfront fashion, even while discussing every single imaginable topic, from Surrealism to technology, from Islamic philosophy to repression and Gulags in the Soviet Union.[1]

His complete works are published in Spanish in a dozen-plus set of hefty volumes. Yet not a single poem by Paz, not an essay or monograph deals with the Jews in general, let alone those in the Hispanic world. This is peculiar because he grew up in Mexico City's middle class, which had a small yet economically vibrant Jewish community. Jews were also active in the arts, from literature to painting to movies and theater. When Paz discusses their contribution, he never highlights their Jewish identity.

The same might be said of another Nobel Prize winner, Gabriel García Márquez (1927–2014), though in his case, the silence is less troublesome because Gabo, as he was known to friends, didn't set out to produce an oeuvre that serves as a map of intellectual affinities. Minorities play a role in his fiction but only those he was personally acquainted with and defined by. The town of Macondo in *One Hundred Years of Solitude* prominently features gypsies as well as foreigners who come following an economic boom. And Arabs are also present. (Gabo's wife Mercedes, aka Meche, of Lebanese descent, serves as the inspiration for one of the female characters.)

And in *Chronicle of a Death Foretold* (1981), Arabs again appear. Their presence is a reflection of the demographic landscape of the Caribbean coast of Colombia, specifically in Aracataca, where the author was born, and in Barranquilla and Cartagena, where he spent his formative years and became a journalist. There were no Jews in the region then, only—or almost only—in the country's major cities, Bogotá and Cali. Thus, it would have been an anachronism, in Gabo's realistic oeuvre, to feature a minority, religious or cultural, he hadn't been exposed to. Unlike the case of Borges's Argentina, his universe wasn't defined by Jews.

Interest is more palpable in other Latin American literary luminaries of the twentieth century. For instance, Julio Cortázar (1914–1984), the Argentine author of *Hopscotch* (1963), delves into the theme of repression and the *desaparecidos* during the *Guerra Sucia*, the Dirty War in Argentina, in his story "Press Clippings," part of *We Love Glenda So Much* (1984). In contrast, Carlos Fuentes (1928–2012), from Mexico, was, throughout his life, far more interested in Jewish topics. Novels such as *A*

Change of Skin (1968) dealt with the Nazis and the Holocaust; *The Hydra Head* (1978), with the Arab-Israeli conflict; and *Terra Nostra* (1975) is an epic—e.g., encyclopedic—retelling of how Hispanic civilization came to be, with the Jews at the heart of *La Convivencia* in the Iberian Peninsula before 1492 and an itinerant life after it up to the twentieth century.

And Mario Vargas Llosa (b.1936), also a Nobel Prize recipient, has featured Jewish characters in his fiction and nonfiction. His novel *The Storyteller* (1987), about a Jewish anthropologist in Lima who becomes a griot among the Machiguenga tribe in the Amazon, and he has also, in his sustained nonfiction career, debated issues such as anti-Semitism and the Arab-Israeli conflict. As an essayist, Vargas Llosa has also written about the Israeli-Palestinian conflict on a number of occasions, including a book-length reportage called *Israel/Palestina: Paz of Guerra Santa* (*Israel/Palestine: Peace or Holy War, 2006*), with photographs by his daughter Morgana.

There are other important figures in Latin American literature, scores of them women: Elena Poniatowska (b.1932), Isabel Allende (b.1942), and Zoé Valdés (b.1959). Some address Jewish topics, others don't. Unquestionably, the authors I discussed in the preceding paragraphs were among the most prominent in the region when Borges became a staple of world literature. He was their acknowledged inspiration, often their primary one. García Márquez, for instance, said that reading Borges—whose books, printed in Argentina, were not distributed in Colombia, which meant the same used copies circulated among devoted friends—made a big impact on his worldview, to the extent that *One Hundred Years of Solitude* wouldn't have been shaped without it. (It is built around a palimpsest, one of Borges's favorite devises.) Cortázar reminisced about Borges reading one of his stories, "House Taken Over," and publishing it in the magazine *Anales de Buenos Aires*. Fuentes described the author of "The Aleph" as the most original of all writers from Latin America and Vargas Llosa as the one with an assured posterity.

This fascination was multifaceted. The Jewish component was small in the Borgesian universe. For these writers it didn't become an entry door to a broader interest on Jewish history, religion, and culture.

In contrast, Borges was interested in Jews, but not as flesh-and-bones people, overwhelmed with ideological interests, religious fervor, and personal passions, but as abstractions. He was attracted to Jews as metaphors. This doesn't mean he didn't socialize with them. While in Geneva and Spain during World War I, he befriended a number of Jews with Polish Jewish origin, among them Maurice Abramowicz (about whom he wrote a poem in 1984) and as Simón Jichlinski. They were "my two bosom friends," Borges wrote in *The New Yorker*. "One became a lawyer and the other a physician. I taught them to play *truco*, and they learned so well and fast that at the end of our first game they left me without a cent." He also became close to Rafael Cansinos-Assens, the latter a Sephardic author responsible for *El candelabro de los siete brazos*. But what attracted him was the Jew as symbol.

This obsession starts with *The Zohar*, the canonical text in Kabbalah. His knowledge on this area came from secondary sources, such as *Jewish Magic and Superstition* by Joshua Trachtenberg, *The Holy Kabbalah* by Arthur E. Waite, and *La Kabbale* by Henri Sérouya, as well as texts by Adolphe Franck and Knorr von Rosenroth, and the entry on the subject in the *Encyclopedia Britannica*. Borges liked the concept of Sephirot, the method of Gematria, and the idea, expounded by Jewish mystics, that language antecedes the creation of the world.

While on a trip to Israel to receive the Jerusalem Prize, Borges was asked what he wanted to see. "Don't ask me what I want to see because I am blind," he responded. "But if you ask me whom I want to see I'll answer, right away, [Gershom]

Scholem. I spent a beautiful afternoon in his house. We met a couple of times. A charming person. He speaks perfect English." Shortly after, Borges wrote a poem about the Golem. The word *Golem* in Spanish is impossible to rhyme—unless, of course, it is matched with Scholem. Herein the first three stanzas in the translation of Alan S. Trueblood, included in Alexander Coleman's *Selected Poems* (1999):

> If, as the Greek maintains in the *Cratylus*,
> A name is the archetype of a thing,
> The rose is in the letters that spell rose
> And the Nile entire resounds in its name's ring.
>
> So, composed of consonants and vowels,
> There must exist one awe-inspiring word
> That God inheres in—that, when spoken, holds
> Almightiness in syllables unslurred.
>
> Adam knew it in the Garden, so did the stars.
> The rusty work of sin, so the cabbalists say,
> Obliterated it completely;
> No generation has found it to this day.

Borges places the myth of the Golem in the kabbalistic tradition. He's interested in the power of the Hebrew language, which, according to legend, was created by God even before the universe came into being. The Argentine pays attention to the Saussurian relationship between object and word. He then uses his stanzas to describe the creation of the Golem by the Maharal of Prague, the magician whose real name was Judah Loew.

> One memory stands out, unlike the rest—
> Dim shapes always fading from time's dim log.
> Still fresh and green the memory persists
> Of Judah Loew, a rabbi once in Prague.

Thirsty to know things only known to God,
Judah Loew shuffled letters endlessly,
Trying them out in subtle combination
Till at last he uttered the name that is the key,

the Gate, the Echo, the Landlord, and the Mansion,
over a dummy which, with fingers wanting grace,
he fashioned, thinking to teach it the arcane
of Words and Letters and Times and Space.

The simulacrum lifted its drowsy lids
And, much bewildered, took in color and shape
In a floating world of sounds. Following this,
It hesitantly took a timid step.

Little by little it found itself, like us,
Caught in the reverberating weft
Of After, Before, Yesterday, meanwhile, Now,
You, Me, Those, the Others, Right and Left.

That cabbalist who played at being God
Gave his spacey offspring the nickname Golem.
(In a learned passage of his volume,
these truths have been conveyed to us by Scholem.)[1]

Borges discovered Kabbalah at an early age. In the conversation with Alazraki, which took place at Buenos Aires's National Library, he suggested his interest was sparked by Dante's *Divine Comedy* and by his adolescent readings of the *Encyclopedia Britannica*:

> I found it in Longfellow's translation of the *Divine Comedy* which he undertook during the Civil war to avoid thinking about the war he was too preoccupied with. There is a three-page appendix in that translation that Longfellow took from a book—I

believe it was *Rabbinical Literature*—by J. P. Stehelin where there is a discussion of the Hebrew alphabet and of the different meanings and values that the Kabbalists attributed to those letters. And the other reference must have come from the *Britannica*. As a youngster, I used to come here, to the Library, quite frequently, and since I was very shy and didn't dare ask the librarian for books, I would take a volume of the *Britannica*, any volume, from the shelf myself. Since they were readily accessible in the reading room, I did not have the request of any librarian, so I would take a volume and read it. But the old *Encyclopedia Britannica* was far superior to the more recent editions. It used to be a reading work, and now it has been turned into a reference book. I remember one afternoon, one evening, I felt happy because I read articles on . . . [pause], wait, on *Druids*, *Druses*, and then it came—the article on *Dryden*.

Later, Borges stated:

Dante, referring to Virgil, says *il lungo studio e il grande amore*, I think, my Italian is not to be trusted; in my case, I cannot talk about *a long love*, but I can certainly talk about *a long study* of the Kabbalah, because that study was real. Regarding my inclinations toward the study, it was—I think—a double source. To begin with, all things Jewish have always fascinated me and I think this was due to the fact that my maternal grandmother was a Protestant—an Anglican. She knew her Bible, so much so that if somebody quoted a verse, any verse, she would reply: yes, *Job*, such and such chapter and verse, or *Kings*, such and such chapter and verse. So that there was that side. And then, since I have not been able to believe in a personal God, the idea of a vast and

> impersonal god, the *En-Sof* of the Kabbalah, has always fascinated me. Later on, I have found the same, well, in Spinoza, and in pantheism in general, and also in Schopenhauer, and in Samuel Butler, and in Bernard Shaw's idea of "Life's force," and Bergson's "élan vital." All that responded to the same attraction. There is, in addition, a more circumstantial factor. The first book I read in German, when I was studying German by myself, around 1916, was Meyrink's novel, *Der Golem.* I was sent on the study of German by my reading of Carlyle whom I greatly admired. (Now I find his style more intimidating than persuasive.) I started by the same foolish thing many people do, by trying to read Kant's *Critique of Pure Reason* in German, a book not even Germans understand, and which very few people comprehend. Then a friend of mine—what was her name?—she was a baroness from Prague, wait, oh yes, Baroness Forschtübber, she told me that a very interesting book had just been published, a fantastic novel entitled *Der Golem.* I had never heard that word before. That was the first work in German I read through—the first book in prose, since I had earlier read Heine's *Lyrisches Intermezzo.*[2]

Borges's first piece on the Kabbalah is called "A Defense of the Kabbalah." It was first published in *Discusión* (1932). His style at the time was still unformed.

> Neither the first time it has been attempted, nor the last time it will fail, this defense is distinguished by two facts. One is my almost complete ignorance of the Hebrew language; the other, my desire to defend not the doctrine but rather the hermeneutical or cryptographic procedures that lead to it. These procedures, as is well known, include the vertical reading of sacred

> texts, the reading referred to as *boustrophedon* (one line from left to right, the following line from right to left), the methodical substitution of certain letters of the alphabet for others, the sum of the numerical value of the letters, etc. To ridicule such operations is simple; I prefer to attempt to understand them.

Borges talks about the Kabbalah itself indirectly. His mission is to discuss the divine nature of the Holy Scriptures as understood by Christians and Muslims. He isn't interested in religion but in the fact that "the Spirit" creates the universe, that is, turns Himself into a Creator. But his interest in literature, and thus:

> Let us imagine now this astral intelligence, dedicated to manifesting itself not in dynasties or annihilations or birds, but in written words. Let us also imagine, according to the pre-Augustinian theory of verbal inspiration, that God dictates, word by word, what he proposes to say. This premise (which was the one postulated by the Kabbalists) turns the Scriptures into an absolute text, where the collaboration of chance is calculated at zero. The conception alone of such a document is a greater wonder than those recorded in its pages. A book impervious to contingencies, a mechanism of infinite purposes, of infallible variations, of revelations lying in wait, of superimpositions of light. . . . How could one not only study it to absurdity, to numerical excess, as did the Kabbalah?[3]

Throughout his life, Borges used a number of kabbalistic motifs, sometimes overtly, others in a tangential, even subliminal fashion. "The Circular Ruins," for instance, might be read as a tribute to the myth of the Golem. In the story a magician who has never had a child decides to dream his own son. Night after night he shapes his successor, until the creation acquires its own life. Then there is "The Aleph," arguably Borges's most emblematic—and famous—tale. The leitmotif behind it isn't the *Zohar* but the Divine Comedy. The protagonist, Borges himself, is in love with a deceased female named Beatriz. He has a rivalry with another writer, Dante Argentino Daneri, who is awarded a prize Borges believes he himself deserves. Daneri invites Borges to visit a basement in his Buenos Aires house where a magical object, "The Aleph," is found. The descent allows the narrator to sense a journey before him.

The fact that the story, and the mysterious object it describes, is called after the first letter of the Hebrew alphabet is a testament to Borges's passion for Jewish culture. The climactic moment in which the narrator is finally in front of "The Aleph" is nothing short of stunning. The staccato rhythm with which the words "I saw" (in Spanish, *ví*) are repeated is an attempt to recreate the simultaneity, or lack thereof, of the coalescing universe. This is Di Giovanni's rendition:

> On the back part of the step, toward the right, I saw a small iridescent sphere of almost unbearable brilliance. At first I thought it was revolving; then I realized that this movement was an illusion created by the dizzying world it bounded. The Aleph's diameter was probably little more than an inch, but all space was there, actual and undiminished. Each thing (a mirror's face, let us say) was infinite things, since I distinctly saw it from every angle of the universe. I saw the teeming sea; I saw daybreak and nightfall; I saw the multitudes of America; I saw a silvery cobweb in the center of a black pyramid; I saw a splintered labyrinth (it was London); I saw, close up, unending eyes watching themselves in me as in a mirror; I saw

all the mirrors on earth and none of them reflected me; I saw in a backyard of Soler Street the same tiles that thirty years before I'd seen in the entrance of a house in Fray Bentos; I saw bunches of grapes, snow, tobacco, lodes of metal, steam; I saw convex equatorial deserts and each one of their grains of sand; I saw a woman in Inverness whom I shall never forget; I saw her tangled hair, her tall figure, I saw the cancer in her breast; I saw a ring of baked mud in a sidewalk, where before there had been a tree; I saw a summer house in Adrogué and a copy of the first English translation of Pliny—Philemon Holland's—and all at the same time saw each letter on each page (as a boy, I used to marvel that the letters in a closed book did not get scrambled and lost overnight); I saw a sunset in Querétaro that seemed to reflect the color of a rose in Bengal; I saw my empty bedroom; I saw in a closet in Alkmaar a terrestrial globe between two mirrors that multiplied it endlessly; I saw horses with flowing manes on a shore of the Caspian Sea at dawn; I saw the delicate bone structure of a hand; I saw the survivors of a battle sending out picture postcards; I saw in a showcase in Mirzapur a pack of Spanish playing cards; I saw the slanting shadows of ferns on a greenhouse floor; I saw tigers, pistons, bison, tides, and armies; I saw all the ants on the planet; I saw a Persian astrolabe; I saw in the drawer of a writing table (and the handwriting made me tremble) unbelievable, obscene, detailed letters, which Beatriz had written to Carlos Argentino; I saw a monument I worshipped in the Chacarita cemetery; I saw the rotted dust and bones that had once deliciously been Beatriz Viterbo; I saw the circulation of my own dark blood; I saw the coupling of love and the modification of death; I saw the Aleph from every point and

> angle, and in the Aleph I saw the earth and in the earth the Aleph and in the Aleph the earth; I saw my own face and my own bowels; I saw your face; and I felt dizzy and wept, for my eyes had seen that secret and conjectured object whose name is common to all men but which no man has looked upon—the unimaginable universe.[4]

Maybe this is the *summa judaica*: the loci where Borges synthesized his obsession in *lo judío*, where he paid his debt to a life-long fascination. Maybe "The Aleph" is his true, his delayed response to the critics of *Crisol* that accused him of being a Judeophile. Maybe this is his best paragraph. Maybe this is the vortex on which his entire oeuvre stands. And maybe—just maybe—this is why the Spanish language exists, or at least this is its justification: a list of lists that makes the world incredibly large as well as frighteningly small.

Borges also wrote a series of sonnets about Spinoza, whom he admired for his geometrical disquisitions on the divine. The first one belongs to *The Self and the Other* (1968). This translation is by Willis Barnstone:

> Here in the twilight the translucent hands
> Of the Jew polishing the crystal glass.
> The dying afternoon is cold with bands
> Of fear. Each day the afternoons all pass
> The same. The hands and space of hyacinth
> Paling in the confines of the ghetto walls
> Barely exists for the quiet man who stalls
> There, dreaming up a brilliant labyrinth.
> Fame doesn't trouble him (that reflection of
> Dreams in the dream of another mirror), nor love,
> The timid love women. Gone the bars,
> He's free, from metaphor and myth, to sit
> Polishing a stubborn lens: the infinite
> Map of the One who now is all His stars.[5]

The second sonnet is called "Baruch Spinoza." It appears in *The Iron Coin* (1976). This translation is also by Barnstone:

> A haze of gold, the Occident lights up
> The window. Now, the assiduous manuscript
> Is waiting, weighed down with the infinite.
> Someone is building God in a dark cup.
> A man engenders God. He is a Jew
> With saddened eyes and lemon-colored skin;
> Time carries him the way a leaf, dropped in
> A river, is borne off by waters to
> Its end. No matter. The magician moved
> Carves out his God with fine geometry;
> From his disease, from nothing, he's begun
> To construct God, using the word. No one
> Is granted such prodigious love as he:
> The love that has no hope of being loved.[6]

Another story where the Hebrew alphabet serves as map is "Death and the Compass." It was published in *Sur* in 1942, and later gathered in *Artifices* (1944). It became part of *Ficciones* (also 1944). In his forward to *Artifices*, translated by Andrew Hurley in *Collected Fictions*, Borges writes:

> Two of [the stories], perhaps, merit some comment: "Death and the Compass" and "Funes, His Memory." The second is a long metaphor for insomnia. The first, in spite of the Germanic or Scandinavian names in it, takes place in a Buenos Aires of dreams: the twisting "rue de Toulon" is the Paseo de Julio; "Triste-le-Roy" is the hotel where Herbert Ashe received, yet probably did not read, the eleventh volume of an imaginary encyclopedia. After this fiction was written, I thought it might be worthwhile to expand the time and space the story covers: the revenge might be bequeathed to others, the periods of time might be calculated in

> years, perhaps in centuries; the first letter of the Name might be uttered in Iceland, the second in Mexico, the third in Hindustan. Is there any need for me to say that there are saints among the Hasidim, and that the sacrifice of four lives in order to obtain the four letters that the Name demands is a fantasy dictated by the shape of my story?[7]

The story "Death and the Compass," inspired by Spinoza, takes place in a European city much like Amsterdam and might be approached as a tacit tribute to one of its illustrious citizens, Baruch Spinoza. After all, this is a detective story with a geometrical plan. The detective is Erik Lönnrot and his nemesis is Red Scharlach. (Notice the redness of the names.)

Lönnrot is invited to exercise his intelligence by sorting out a series of four murders, each committed within symmetrical coordinates of time and space (December 3, January 3, February 3, etc., in the northern part of the city, the western part, etc.). The victims are all Jews: Dr. Marcelo Yarmolinsky, Daniel Simón Azevedo (the last name is Borges's, too), Ginzberg or Ginsburg, etc. He comes across a book by one Lausden called *Philologus hebræogræcus* (1739). The victims are at times Hasidim—one of them has an octavo volume about the teachings of Israel Ba'al Shem Ṭov—or others simply taxi drivers. Lönnrot gets information from a journalist of the *Yiddische Zeitung* about the Tetragrammaton, the four-lettered divine name: *YHVH*. After each murder, a sign appears: "*The first letter of the Name has been written.*"

Red Scharlach, also known as Scharlach the Dandy, was a criminal who "had sworn upon his honor to kill Lönnrot, but Lönnrot never allowed himself to be intimidated. He thought of himself as a reasoning machine, an Auguste Dupin, but there was something of the adventurer in him, even something of the gambler." Eventually Lönnrot realizes a fourth murder is to take place in a precise time and place: March 3, at the abandoned Villa Triste-le-Roy. He has suspected that maybe Red Scharlach might be the last victim but then dismisses the idea. When he arrives, he sees Scharlach. Lönnrot asks: "Scharlach—*you* are looking for the secret name?" Hurley's translation:

> Scharlach stood there, impassive. He had not participated in the brief struggle, and now moved only to put out his hand for Lönnrot's revolver. But then he spoke, and Lönnrot heard in his voice a tired triumphance, a hatred as large as the universe, a sadness no smaller than that hatred.
>
> "No," he said. "I am looking for something more fleeting and more perishable than that—I am looking for Erik Lönnrot."

Scharlach explains how he carefully executed each and every one of his third crimes. He realizes he's about to die. He considers the three symmetrical crimes:

> "There are three lines too many in your labyrinth," he said at last. "I know of a Greek labyrinth that is but one straight line. So many philosophers have been lost upon that line that a mere detective might be pardoned if he became lost as well. When you hunt me dawn in another avatar of our lives, Scharlach, I suggest that you fake (or commit) one crime at A, a second crime at B, eight kilometers from A, then a third crime at C, four kilometers from A and B and halfway between them. Then wait for me at D, two kilometers from A and C, once again halfway between them. Kill me at D, as you are about to kill me at Triste-le-Roy."
>
> "The next time I kill you," Scharlach replied, "I promise you the labyrinth that consists of a single straight line that is invisible and endless."
>
> He stepped back a few steps. Then, very carefully, he fired.[8]

Moving on to other Jewish symbols, Borges was the first, and for a while the only, supporter of Kafka in the Hispanic world, where his style wasn't embraced until well after World War II. Figures such as Felisberto Hernández, Virgilio Piñera, Calvert Casey, and César Aira (perhaps even Julio Cortázar), all Kafkesque in style (meaning obtuse, "weird," illogical in their worldview), are today an essential feature. In an essay called "Kafka and His Precursors," published in 1951 and included in *Other Inquisitions* (1952), in Eliot Weinberger's rendition, Borges writes:

> At one time I considered writing a study of Kafka's precursors. I had thought, at first, that he was as unique as the phoenix of rhetorical praise; after spending a little time with him, I felt I could recognize his voice, or his habits, in the texts of various literatures and various ages. I will note a few of them here, in chronological order.

Rather than offer a hermeneutic interpretation of Kafka, the essay then concentrates on a catalogue of echoes: Zeno's paradox against motion, a fable by the ninth-century Chinese author Han Yu, Kierkegaard, the anti-Semite Léon Bloy, and Lord Dunsany. Borges concludes:

> If I am not mistaken, the heterogeneous pieces I have listed resemble Kafka; if I am not mistaken, not all of them resemble each other. This last fact is what is most significant. Kafka's idiosyncrasy is present in each of those writings, to a greater or lesser degree, but if Kafka had not written, we would not perceive it; that is to say, it would not exist. The poem "Fears and Scruples" by Robert Browning prophesizes the work of Kafka, but our reading of Kafka noticeably refines and diverts our reading of

> the poem. Browning did not read it as we read it now. The word "precursor" is indispensable to the vocabulary of criticism, but one must try to purify it from any connotation of polemic or rivalry. The fact is that each writer *creates* his precursors. His work modifies our conception of the past, as well as it will modify the future. In this correlation, the identity or plurality of men doesn't matter. The first Kafka of "*Betrachtung*" is less a precursor of the Kafka of the gloomy myths and terrifying institutions than is Browning or Lord Dunsany.[9]

The conclusion serves as confirmation of Borges's need to see literature globally. He refuses to approach Kafka in the context of Jewish literature exclusively. He doesn't even mention his Czech origins and his German-language style. What matters to him are the reverberations of Kafka's motifs. Borges is interested in the Kafka of the Hassidic parables, not in the novelist of *The Metamorphosis* and *The Castle*.

Still, in 1943, he introduced, for Editorial Losada in Buenos Aires, Kafka's *La metamorfosis*. A few years earlier he talked about him (and about Max Brod) in *El Hogar* (July 8, 1938). Borges also included material by Kafka in his *Anthology of Fantastic Literature* (1940), co-edited with Adolfo Bioy Casares and Silvina Ocampo, as well as in his compendia *Libro del cielo y del infierno* (1960, also with Bioy Casares), *Libro de los seres imaginarios* (1967), and *Libro de sueños* (1976). Third and fourth pieces by Borges on Kafka were in the form of introductions. The third was the fourth title of *A Personal Library*, Borges's last editorial project, published between 1985 and 1986 in Argentina and Spain by Emecé and in Italian by Franco Marco Ricci. His selection included *Amerika* and some short stories. The fourth piece is a prologue he wrote toward the end of his life, as part of a project called *The Library of Babel* paid by the publisher Ediciones Siruela in Spain from 1978 to 1986. The volumes were designed to be short. They were fantastic tales selected by Borges. From Kafka he chose *The Vulture*. The book appeared in 1979. The prologue offers fresh views on Borges's opinion not only on the author but on Jews in general. Herein some random thoughts:

> Everyone knows that Kafka always felt mysteriously guilty toward his father, in the manner of Israel with its God; his Judaism, which separated him from the rest of mankind, affected him in a complex way. The consciousness of approaching death and the feverish exaltation of tuberculosis must have sharpened those faculties. . . .
>
> Two ideas—or more exactly, two obsessions—rule Kafka's work: subordination and the infinite. In almost all his fictions there are hierarchies, and those hierarchies are infinite. . . .
>
> The most unquestionable virtue of Kafka is the invention of intolerable situations. A few lines are enough to indelibly demonstrate. For example: "the animal sizes the whip from the hands of its master and beats him in order to become the master and doesn't realize that this is nothing but an illusion produced by a new knot in the whip." Or: "Leopards invade the temples and drink wine from the chalices; this happens suddenly; in the end it was foreseen that this would happen and it is incorporated into the liturgy." The elaboration, in Kafka, is less admirable than the invocation.[10]

A less overt, yet equally significant, tribute to Kafka appears in the story "The Secret Miracle," barely six to seven pages in length. Like "*Deutsches Requiem*," it has a single, unifying argument: the last hours of a prisoner about to be executed by the Nazis; and the two focus on a single concept, although from different perspectives: self-redemption. The former has a Jew as its protagonist, but it is narrated from by an omniscient third-person narrator; the latter, instead, has a Nazi as its main character, and it is he who delivers the tale to us.

But let me discuss them in detail, so as to highlight their similarities and, also, to announce a philosophy of life and art that emerges from them. "The Secret Miracle," written during World War II and collected in *Ficciones*, forms a triptych with Borges's other Jewish tales: "Emma Zunz" and "Death and the Compass." (I included the three in the anthology *Tropical Synagogues* [1994], revised as *Oy Caramba! An Anthology of Jewish Stories from Latin America* [2016]). It is more than a subliminal tribute to one Kafka, dead by then for approximately a couple of decades.

The story opens with an epigraph from the *Qur'an*, 2:261: "And God caused him to die for an hundred years, and the raised him to life. And God said, 'How long hast thou waited?' He said, 'I have waited a day or part of a day.'" Borges sets the plot in Prague in 1943. In the first scene Jaromir Hladik, a translator and playwright arrested by the Nazis for being Jewish, is taken to prison. The first scene is emblematic: it describes a dream Hladik has of a long chess game in which the opponents had been at each other for such an extent of time, they had forgotten what the prize was to be. Even the rules of the game had been forgotten. Hladik was the first born of one of the families. Clearly, Borges is setting the stage for a rivalry between Jews and Nazis as ancient as the world itself.

It is in his cell where Hladik communicates with God and this communication is the centripetal force in the argument. Hladik, we find out, is the author an unfinished drama called *The Enemies* and he knows that, if his life is to have any meaning, it is because of his authorship of this drama. So he requests that God grant him a miracle—a secret miracle, since only he and he alone will know about it. In the final scene, as Hladik faces a German firing squad, the universe comes to a stop:

> The guns converged on Hladik, but the men who were to kill him stood motionless. The sergeant's arm eternized an unfinished gesture. On a paving stone of the courtyard a bee cast an unchanging shadow. The wind had ceased, as in a picture. . . . He had asked God for a whole year to finish his work; His omnipotence had granted it. God had worked a secret miracle for him; German lead would kill him at the set hour, but in his mind a year would go by between the order and its execution.[11]

In the very last line, Borges has Hladik is shot to death on March 29, at 9:02 a.m. Even though no evidence of a finished manuscript of *The Enemies* can be found, the prisoner dies satisfied: his life has been justified. Its justification has to do with immortality. Borges's statement is clear: a writer's raison d'être is to leave behind the better part of his talent, and to struggle so that that contribution is finished, even if only "ideally." It is clear, to me at least, that in the face of tyranny and death, the Argentine understood what Jews in Europe were about: faith, endurance, and posterity.

~

Another modern Jewish writer attracting Borges's interest, albeit with considerably less enthusiasm, was Agnon, aka Shmuel Yosef Czaczkes (1887–1970). Their connection has been studied far less in his oeuvre. In the mid-sixties, Borges delivered a couple of lectures at the Instituto Cultural Argentino-Israelí in Buenos Aires, one on the *Book of Job*, the other on Spinoza. These lectures were eventually translated into English. A chance remark to Neal Sokol—included in *Ilan Stavans: Eight Conversations* (2004)—in which I state that Borges never read Shmuel Yosef Agnon, prompted a Canadian friend, Carl Rosenberg, editor of *Outlook*, to send me, so as to correct my ignorance, a third, significantly shorter lecture by Borges, previously unknown even to specialists. It was delivered at the same institution in 1967, approximately a year after Agnon was awarded the Nobel Prize, which he shared with the German poet Nelly Sachs.

In "On Sh. Y. Agnon," which I hereby reconstruct in English (the Spanish transcription is awful), Borges mentions, in passing, Agnon's edition of the *Tales the Ba'al Shem-Tov*. He also refers to *Days of Awe*, which Schocken issued in 1965 in the United States, under the supervision of Nahum Glatzer, with one of those elongated subtitles more suitable for poetry slams than for libraries: "being a treasury of traditions, legends and learned commentaries concerning Rosh ha-Shanah, Yom Kippur and the days between, culled from three hundred volumes, ancient and new." But as the nonbeliever he was—and even less of an enthusiast of religious rituals—Borges prefers *Contes de Jérusalem* (1959), which he read in the French rendition of Rachel and Guy Casaril. The anthology includes nine of Agnon's tales, among them "Forevermore," "Tehila," "The Whole Loaf," "Ido and Enam," and "Orange Peel: A Fantasy."

> I begin with some considerations that run the risk of appearing digressive but which should take us to the essential theme: the personality and oeuvre of our great contemporary, Shmuel Yosef Agnon. My ignorance of Hebrew—ignorance which I deplore but which it's late to remedy it—has forced me to judge him through *Days of Awe*, about the Jewish liturgical year; and *Contes de Jérusalem*. I'll limit myself to the astonishment I've experienced in these volumes, the latter especially.
>
> Let me ask a simple yet complex question, which is what all questions are: What is a nation? My first reaction is to offer a geographical answer but it would be insufficient. Instead, let us envision a nation as the series of memories stored at the heart

of a people. George Bernard Shaw was once asked: How much suffering is humankind able to bear? His answer was that the suffering of a single individual is enough and is also the limit. In other words, the limit might be an abstraction, although the suffering itself is real. And so, if misery is impossible to measure in collective terms, how might one define a nation?

To me there isn't a clearer example of a nation than Israel, whose origins are almost confused with those of the world entire, and who reaches us today after much misery and exile. A nation is made of the accumulated memory of successive generations. In itself, memory is often approached in a couple of ways: as a barren collection of dates, names and locations; and as a catalog of curiosities. But there's another approach neither endorsed by historians, nor by students of folklore: memory as experience incarnated in people. This, precisely, is what I find in Agnon.

Contes de Jérusalem ought to be read like one reads Dante: as a series of tales, at once tragic and humorous; and as a set of symbols. Agnon enables us to appreciate ancient Jewish tradition through a game of mirrors. In it he also invites to recognize the role of Hasidism. Unquestionably, the Hasidic tales compiled by Martin Buber and, in his early years, by Agnon too, left an indelible imprint on him. For instance, "Ido and Enam," filled with mystery, is the bizarre tale of a scholar who, in an act of revelation, sees ninety-nine words of an unknown language. Ninety-nine are also the names of God; the Tetragrammaton, which is the hundredth one, is infallible. Indirectly, Agnon recalls in his pages the legend of the Golem, made out of sand by means of words by a Cabalist in Prague's Jewish quarter.

I shall now refer to "The Whole Loaf," a story about chance. It reminds me of Kafka, who is part of Jewish memory too. Agnon chronicles the infinite yet minuscule obstacles undergone by its hungry protagonist as he prepares for the Sabbath. Whereas Kafka was about the lack of hope, or else about a hope so remote it generates in us a terrible feeling of desperation, Agnon is patient: he waits because he's a believer. Indeed, one of the right decisions the Swedish Academy made recently was not to award its Nobel Prize to a writer of sadness and despair. Instead, it honored one who, like Bernard Shaw, also a laureate, is sensitive to tragedy but knows that a joyful conclusion to the human quest isn't altogether beyond us.

Another story in *Contes de Jérusalem* is about a country that could be any country. This one in particular is punished with a drought marked by an inexorably blue sky. Furthermore, enemies are always on the attack, the earth is barren and rivers are empty. The population is divided into two parties: on one side are the cover-headed, on the other the naked-headed. . . . The two parties are ready to destroy each other. Yet there's a single individual who is beyond any affiliation. He furtively leaves the city, praying for God to send a compassionate storm to stop the destruction. When the others find out, they excommunicate him. His sin: not to have alerted the authorities to his wishes. A decision is then made to have everyone build a huge tent for protection from the storm, which must be large enough to cover the entire country. A commission is established to decide what name to give to the tent. Alternative commissions take the responsibility of studying the etymology and orthography of the chosen name. As

> the population wastes its energy in trivialities, God allows rain to fall—and the barren land is fertilized, just as modern Israel itself was fertilized. I hear a distant echo in Agnon's story of the Jewish tradition that says that every generation includes a total of thirty-six just men. By the way, this tradition was studied by Max Brod, Kafka's friend. Unacquainted with one another, these just men navigate the world and are replaced as soon as they die. Right now their dynasty redeems us.
>
> Israel's memory is in Agnon—not an erudite but a living memory. He is known through a pseudonym; he didn't write for his own vanity. Somehow he knew he was the living memory of that admirable people to which, beyond the vicissitudes of blood, we all belong: the people of Israel.[12]

The interest in Agnon is part of Borges's admiration for Israel as a young nation. His relationship with the Jewish state was ambivalent at first, and only in later years—when he himself became an institutional luminary—did he soften his approach to it. It isn't that Borges was critical of Zionism. In fact, judging by his work, he seems to have had a limited knowledge of it. International politics didn't interest him in the least. He seldom talked about Theodor Herzl, nor even about Eliezer ben Yehuda, credited for the modern revival of the Hebrew language.

Borges visited Israel twice. The first trip came at the invitation of Prime Minister David Ben-Gurion. It was in recognition of his philo-Semitism, and in particular of his positive views on Israel. He had been active in the Casa Argentina en Israel-Tierra Santa, a project that sought to create an Argentine cultural center in Jerusalem. He also was the first to write in *Sur* (no. 254, September-October 1958). In the "An Autobiographical Essay," done in collaboration of Norman Thomas Di Giovanni, Borges stated:

Early in 1969, invited by the Israeli government, I spent ten very exciting days in Tel Aviv and Jerusalem. I brought home the conviction of having been in the oldest and the youngest of nations, of having come from a very living, vigilant land to a half-asleep nook of the world. Since my Geneva days, I had always been interested in Jewish culture, thinking of it as an integral element of our so-called Western civilization, and during the Israeli-Arab war of a few years back I found myself taking immediate sides. While the outcome was still uncertain, I wrote a poem on the battle. A week later, I wrote another on the victory. Israel was, of course, still an armed camp at the time of my visit. There, along the shores of Galilee, I kept recalling these lines from Shakespeare:

> Over whose acres walk'd those blessed feet,
> Which fourteen hundred years ago, were nail'd
> For our advantage, on the bitter cross.[13]

Actually, there are a total of three poems in Borges's collection *In Praise of Darkness* (1969). All were later included in his *Obras Completas*. I don't believe these poems have been rendered into English. Herein my versions. First, "To Israel":

> Who shall tell if you, Israel, are to be found
> In the lost labyrinth of secular rivers
> That is my blood? Who shall locate the places
> Where my blood and yours have navigated?
> It doesn't matter. I know you're in the Sacred
> Book that comprehends Time, rescued in history
> By the red Adam, as well as by the memory
> And agony of the Crucified One.
> You're in the Book that is the mirror
> Of each face approaching it,

As well as God's face, which, in its complex
And hard crystal, is appreciated in terror.
Long live Israel, who keeps God's wall
In your passionate battle.

"Israel":

A man incarcerated and bewitched,
a man condemned to be the serpent
that keeps the infamous gold,
a man condemned to be Shylock,
a man wandering through the globe,
knowing he had been in Paradise,
an old and blind man who ought to tear down
the temple columns,
a face condemned to be a mask,
a man who in spite of humankind
is Spinoza and the Ba'al Shem and the Kabbalists,
a man that is a Book,
a mouth praising heaven's justice
from the abyss,
an attorney or a dentist
who talked with God on a mountain,
a man condemned to ridicule
and an abomination, a Jew,
an ancient man,
burnt and drowned in lethal chambers,
an obstinate man who is immortal
and now has returned to battle,
to the violent light of victory,
beautiful like a lion at noon.

And "Israel, 1969":

I feared Israel would be threatened,
with sweet insidiousness,

by the nostalgia that secular diasporas
accumulated, like sorrowful treasure,
in the cities of the infidel, the *juderías*,
the twilight of the steppe, the dreams—
the nostalgia of those who, near the waters of
Babylon,
longed for you, Jerusalem.
What else were you, Israel, if not that nostalgia,
the will to safe-keep,
from the inconstant shapes of time,
your old magical book, your liturgy,
your solitude with God?
I was wrong. The oldest of nations
is also the youngest.
You haven't been tempted by gardens,
otherness and boredom,
but by the rigor of the last frontier.
Israel has announced, without words:
you shall forget who you are—
you shall leave behind your previous self.
You shall forget who you were in those lands
that gave you their afternoons and mornings
and which you shall no longer cherish.
You shall forget your parents' tongue
and learn the tongue of Paradise.
You shall be an Israeli. You shall be a soldier.
You shall build the homeland with swamps,
you shall erect it in deserts.
Your brother shall work with you,
he whose face you haven't seen before.
Only one thing is promised:
your place in the battlefield.[14]

There's a strange, triumphant, pompous (almost unBorgesian) tone and tune to these poems. They eulogize the Six Day War figuratively, in abstract, without placing it in context: The oldest of nations/is also the youngest. Whoever is interested in the Arab-Israeli conflict won't get an uninterested picture though them. Instead, the reader appreciates a blind fervor.

The second time Borges visited Israel was in 1971, to receive the Jerusalem Prize.

He also embraced, though tangentially and, thus, not in a way that significantly influenced his *weltanschauung*, Isaac Babel, another Jewish author with few echoes in the Spanish-speaking world. In a "capsule biography" about him published in 1938 in the magazine *El Hogar*, to which Borges contributed between 1936 and 1939, he portrays Babel, who was still alive at the time, as a defiant Jew. Herein Esther Allen's translation:

> He was born in the jumbled catacombs of the stair-stepped port of Odessa, late in 1894. Irreparably Semitic, Isaac was the son of a rag merchant from Kiev and a Moldavian Jewess. Catastrophe has been the normal climate of his life. In the uneasy intervals between pogroms he learned not only to read and write but to appreciate literature and enjoy the work of Maupassant, Flaubert, and Rabelais. In 1914, he was certified a lawyer by the faculty of Law in Saratov; in 1916, he risked a journey to Petrograd. In that capital city "traitors, malcontents, whiners, and Jews" were banned: the category was somewhat arbitrary, but—implacably—it included Babel. He had to rely on the friendship of a waiter who took him home and hid him, on a Lithuanian accent acquired in Sebastopol, and on an apocryphal passport. His first writings date from that period: two or three satires of the Czarist bureaucracy, published in *Annals*, Gorky's famous newspaper. (What must he think, and not say, about Soviet Russia, that indecipherable labyrinth of state offices?) Those two or three satires attracted the dangerous attention of the government.

> He was accused of pornography and incitement of class hatred. From this catastrophe he was saved by another catastrophe: the Russian Revolution.
>
> In early 1921, Babel joined a Cossack regiment. Those blustering and useless warriors (no one in the history of the universe has been defeated more often than the Cossacks) were, of course, anti-Semitic. The mere idea of a Jew on horseback struck them as laughable, and the fact that Babel was a good horseman only added to their disdain and spite. A couple of well-timed and flashy exploits enabled Babel to make them leave him in peace.
>
> By reputation, though not according to the bibliographies, Isaac Babel is still a *homo unius libri.*
>
> His unmatched book is titled *Red Cavalry*.
>
> The music of its style contrasts with the almost ineffable brutality of certain scenes.
>
> One of the stories—"Salt"—enjoys a glory seemingly reserved for poems, and rarely attained by prose: many people know it by heart.[15]

Years ago, I introduced Isaac Babel's stories to a Spanish-speaking audience. (An English version of the introduction to *Cuentos de Odesa* and *Caballería roja* [1993] appears in my book *The Inveterate Dreamer* [2001].) Borges's profile is a revelation because no two writers could be more different. Indeed, they are like and oil and water: the Russian, while a meticulous stylist á la Maupassant, focused on the physical (e.g., the Jewish body) and on political and social tensions in the early Soviet Union; the Argentine, instead, was an escapist concerned with the metaphysical. Borges's understanding of Babel comes through secondary sources, as did much of his knowledge in general. Still, even if he had read his stories, and I'm skeptical about it, the connection between them would have remained tenuous.

Addendum: Had he read it, I wonder what Borges would have thought of Bruno Schulz's *The Street of Crocodiles* (1934) and *Sanatorium under the Sign of the Hourglass* (1937). And what if Schulz's unfinished novel *The Messiah* had ended up in Buenos Aires, mysteriously found in the desk of Witold Gombrowicz, who nurtured an almost unrivaled envy of Borges?

PART IV

BEYOND TRANSLATION

The original is unfaithful to the translation.

—"On William Beckford's *Vathek*" (1943)

A friend of mine gave me a precious gift: a small anthology of Borges's work translated into Yiddish, published by YIVO (in Spanish, IWO) in Buenos Aires in 1976. Barely thirty pages long, it contains a few poems (including "To Israel" and "The Golem," "The Secret Miracle," and "*Deutsches Requiem*"). Reading it wasn't particularly enlightening yet somehow it made me feel inspired. The existence of such anthology reminded me of an anecdote found in Saul Bellow's travel book *To Jerusalem and Back* (1976). In it he tells of an encounter with Hebrew novelist Sh. Y. Agnon, with whom he talked about a number of topics, including translation.

Agnon asked Bellow if his worked had already been translated into Hebrew. Bellow replied that it had been rendered into other languages but not yet to the Sacred Tongue, which didn't quite bother him since the number of Hebrew speakers then—as now—was small. Ah, replied Agnon, but in Hebrew "it will be saved" for the ages.

No piece of literature was ever "rescued" by being translated into Yiddish. Still, to me Borges in Yiddish feels (or could feel) close to home—almost as close as in the Spanish original. Unfortunately, the translations by Yitskhok Niborski, Mimi Pinzón, and Kahat Klieger aren't, in my opinion, particularly imaginative.

Of all the intellectual exercises Borges engaged in throughout his career, the one that doesn't directly address Jewish themes yet looks to me like a palette in which he reimagined, albeit tangentially, his obsession with his own Jewishness is translation. As a result of their status as outsiders, Jews have played a prominent role as linguistic bridges, either rendering works from one language to another, or else exploring the linguistic conundrum of humankind.

It is fatuous to claim—and I certainly don't have any intention of doing so—that Borges's translations are defined by his interest in things Jewish. On the contrary, they are rather uncontained, a multifarious effort that permeated his entire life and was the result of a genuine hunger for language as a paradox. That paradox is intimately linked to his location as an outsider and to his admiration for translators in general (he constantly praises them in his pages). That attitude distills a sensibility characteristic in Jewish culture.

Up until now, I have addressed the visible signs of his interest in Jewish themes. In this section and the next, I intend to talk about the invisible ones, namely, either about Borges as a practitioner of translation or about his condition as a wandering soul. I won't push the Jewish connections, in part because in the choices I have made to reflect on the topic, Jews play no role. Still, to understand the larger implications of these reflections it is important to keep in mind that sensibility.

In early 1999, I published in the *Times Literary Supplement* a book review of *Collected Fictions*, by Borges, translated by Andrew Hurley. This volume was part of an orchestrated effort by the publisher Viking, and supported of Andrew Wylie Literary Agency, to repackage the oeuvre of the Argentine master in three easily manageable anthologies of fiction, non-fiction, and poetry, respectively. The editorial effort was made to coincide with Borges's centennial. Hurley's was the first of the three anthologies to appear. My essay praised it while also expressing sadness at the realization that Hurley's versions were destined to replace earlier English translations, in particular the admirable ones by Donald A. Yates and James E. Irby in *Labyrinths: Selected Stories and Other Writings* (1964).

The review included a statement that, to my surprise, proved to be considerably controversial, to the effect that the best translations of Borges's oeuvre, not only into Shakespeare's tongue but also into the language of Flaubert and Valéry, might have superseded the originals in quality. I also suggested that, given his early British education in Buenos Aires, to read the Argentine in English is, in a way, "to bring him back home." I invoked the famous fact, stated by Borges in the "An Autobiographical Essay," that he read *Don Quixote* in English first; years later, when stumbling upon Cervantes original, he felt it was a lousy translation.

My comment gave place to an immediate, far-reaching clamor. There was an exchange in the *TLS* correspondence section that lasted several weeks, about these and other aspects of the review and of the editorial effort. It reverberated in other periodicals. Several of Borges's translators, editors, and biographers entered the debate, which was less about the value of Hurley's translations than about the status of the Argentine in twentieth-century literature. In the Spanish-speaking world, on the other hand, the controversy was about "losing" the author of "El Aleph" and *Other Inquisitions* to an "abductor": the English language.

It is this aspect of the polemic that interests me. In Argentina, in the pages of *La Nación* newspaper, a deliberation ensued on the value of reading Borges in a foreign language. Other reactions appeared in Spain and the Americas, in monthlies such as *Cuadernos Hispanoamericanos*. I apparently offended people for whom Borges is "a milestone of Hispanic culture."

To say that he tasted equally good or better in translation than in Spanish amounted to heresy, for instance, by depriving a civilization of a coveted treasure.

I'm not the first to endorse such an apostasy: Martin Amis. J. M. Coetzee, and Salman Rushdie, among others, expressed similar opinions once; but none of them is fully versed in Quevedo's tongue, so their views might be taken as fanciful; in turn, I *come* from *lo español*, at least partially, and translation, the art and act of it, are for me essential, as constitutive as breathing. I have reflected on this aspect of my life in *On Borrowed Words: A Memoir of Language* (2001). My education in Mexico was in three languages: Yiddish, Spanish, and Hebrew; and eventually I embraced a fourth one: English. It is almost impossible for me, at this stage, to establish which, of all, is closest to my heart. Translation, hence, is a daily routine; it is everywhere I go and in everything I do.

And so is literature, which, as far as I'm concerned, has no owner: once it is out and about, it is less the property of the author than of any and all readers. It is said, in James E. Irby's translation, in "Borges and I," on which I reflect at some length in the coda to this volume: "[W]hat is good belongs to no one . . . but rather to the language and to tradition." Is this sentence better than its Spanish counterpart: "*lo bueno ya no es de nadie, ni siquiera del otro, sino del lenguaje o la tradición*"? I delve deeper into this topic in the next section, "On the Language of Ghosts." For now, I have a further question: Does it really matter which of these universes is better than another of equal caliber? To translate, in my view, is to make the particular universal, to enter a Leibnizian reality in which simultaneous universes coexist.

Borges's syntax is revolutionary because, among other reasons, it cleansed Spanish of excesses even the *Modernistas* indulged in, let alone the Symbolists and Parnassianists; he made the Spanish language more precise, succinct, almost mathematical—he made it sound like English. Or else, he made English more accessible, less remote to readers in Buenos Aires, and henceforth the rest of the Hispanic orbit.

As I said, I want to address his obsession with translation, though; it will allow me to explore the tension between original and "replica" in a way that, I hope, is a response to my critics. It dates back to his adolescence: at the age of seven Borges drafted in English a summary of Greek mythology, and a couple of years later he rendered into Spanish "*El príncipe feliz*," a story by Oscar Wilde, and through the help of a relative, published it; readers thought the translation wasn't by him, aka Jorge Borges, but by his father, Jorge Guillermo Borges. This passion, no doubt, persisted throughout his life: translators are protagonists in a myriad of stories of his, from "Pierre Menard, Author of the *Quixote*" and "Averroes' Search" to "The Secret Miracle"; and in essays such as "The Translator of the *1001 Nights*," "The Homeric Versions," and "The Enigma of Edward Fitzgerald," he ponders the role translators play in the *rezeptionsgeshichte* of a book or in the buildup of a heritage.

All this is part of the Argentine's easily *available* oeuvre; there is a less approachable aspect, too. Years ago, I acquired in Manhattan a copy of *Borges: Obras, reseñas y traducciones inéditas. Diario "Crítica," 1933–34*, where many early efforts by Borges to translate international figures into Spanish: G. K. Chesterton, Lafcadio Hearn, Kipling, Dickens, Jack London, George Bernard Shaw, Swift, Wilde, Carl Sandburg, Eugene O'Neill, and T. E. Lawrence (as well as French and German figures such as Marcel Schwob and Gustav Meyrink). Borges was in his mid-thirties at the time and the literary pages of *Crítica* were his to experiment with.

The results are decidedly mixed, but this, to me, is less important than the fact that these experiments took place, for the Argentine was in search of a voice and a viewpoint, and through these translations he found, or at least solidified them. In due time, several non-fiction pieces from *Crítica*, especially from *Revista Multicolor de los Sábados*, made it to his collection

Universal History of Infamy, and one or two of them to *Discusión* and *El hacedor* also. This, of course, doesn't necessarily say anything significant about Borges's view on translation. Scores of litterateurs translate in their free time: for money, most often, but also for posterity.

So what *were* his views? He didn't prepare an *Ars Poetica* on translation; it is preposterous to produce one that simplifies and perverts. In contrast, I suggest four illustrative examples. My first example is about Pierre Menard, who is and isn't a translator of Cervantes. He is indeed described as the author of "a manuscript translation" of Quevedo's *Aguja de navegar cultos* into French under the title *La boussole des précieux*; as well as a translation, with a prologue and notes, of *Libro de la invención liberal y arte del juego del axedrez*. But his version of *Don Quixote* isn't a translation in the strict sense of the term; instead, it is "a rewriting." Might it be implied that, in Borges view, a translation might also be another fresh original?

My second example to spring to mind is a sentence in "On William Beckford's *Vathek*," a line that is a favorite of mine: "The original is unfaithful to the translation." This is a forceful statement: Borges didn't see translations as substitutes, replacements, hand-me-downs; instead, he perceived them—especially the translations of classics such as *The Iliad* and Dante's *Divine Comedy*—as equally, if not more, valuable originals. This desire to experiment with language and to give birth to a text in a particular linguistic realm is evident in his so-called "Two English Poems," drafted in 1934 and dedicated to the improbable Beatriz Babiloni Webster de Bullrich. They are part of *El otro, el mismo* (1964). I quote from the second:

> I offer you my ancestors, my dead men, the ghosts that living men have honoured in marble: my father's father killed in the frontier in Buenos Aires, two bullets through his lungs, bearded and dead, wrapped by his soldiers in the hide of a cow; my mother's grand-

> father—just twenty-four—heading a charge of three hundred men in Peru, now ghosts on vanished horses.
>
> I offer you whatever insights my books may hold, whatever manliness or humour my life.[1]

Echoes of Borges's Spanish poetry abound, but these two are poems *in* English: they were not translated, but delivered in Browning's tongue; and they still inhabit it. (The Argentine included them in his *Obras Completas*.) Only *in English*, too, is his "An Autobiographical Essay."

Another significant example, the third in this sequence, is in "The Translator of *1001 Nights*," published in Spanish in 1935 and collected in *Historia de la eternidad*. In it, the Argentine contrasts the four major translators of *Quitab alif laila ua laila*, as it is known in Arabic: Richard Francis Burton, Edward Lane, Antoine Galland, and J. C. Mardrus. He wonders, for instance, by which process of misappropriation—e.g., mistranslation—the title *Book of the Thousand Nights and One Night* came to be. It is enlightening, in this context, to realize that not a single one of the three Spanish renditions of the book up until the thirties is ever considered.

This is symptomatic: How is it that an erudite, cosmopolitan Spanish-language critic in remote Buenos Aires compares a handful of English, German, and French versions, but never the ones emanating from his milieu? The answer is straightforward: at no time did Borges perceive himself as trapped in the Spanish language; language, after all, isn't a prison but a springboard. As a perfect polyglot, he realized—and seized upon the fact that—his own territory, his milieu was not Argentine letters alone, and Spanish culture in particular, but world literature in its entirety, and every language at his disposal in general.

This, truly, is his outstanding contribution to the topic of translation. Why be imprisoned in our own environment? In "The Argentine Writer and Tradition," in my eyes one of his most significant pieces, he announced:

> I believe our tradition is all of Western culture, and I also believe we have a right to that tradition, greater than that which the inhabitants of one or another Western nation might have. . . . I believe that we Argentines, we South Americans in general . . . can handle all European themes, handle them without superstition, with an irreverence which can have, and already does have, fortunate consequences. . . . Anything we Argentine writers can do successfully will become part of our Argentine tradition, in the same way that the treatment of Italian themes belongs to the tradition of England through the efforts of Chaucer and Shakespeare.[2]

I hereby come to my fourth and last example, about which I have a bit more to say. Beyond the almost two dozen uneven exercises in *Crítica*, Borges's sustained efforts at translation include a cluster of full-fledged books and numerous stories, essays, and aphorisms, commissioned for publications by publishers as self-sufficient volumes or as integral parts of anthologies the Argentine edited alone and in collaboration with Adolfo Bioy Casares and others.

A decade or so ago, in Madrid, I came across in a bookstore his rendition of Virginia Woolf's *Orlando*, as well as his version of her influential essay *A Room of One's Own*, both released in Spanish by Ediciones Sur in 1937, and assigned to Borges by his friend and editor-in-chief of the monthly *Sur*, Victoria Ocampo; I've also held in my hands his translation from the French of André Gide's *Persephone* and Henri Michaux's *A Barbarian in Asia*; and I have in my library his translation of *The Wild Palms*, William Faulkner's novel of 1939.

I have a handful of impressions to offer on the latter. The edition I have of it—*Las palmeras salvajes*, Buenos Aires, Editorial

Sudamericana, 1970, with a prologue by Juan Benet—has a copyright dated in 1962, twenty-three years after Faulkner published its original in English. But the Uruguayan critic and Yale professor Emir Rodríguez Monegal, in his 1978 biography of the Argentine and in an anthology called *Borges: A Reader*, dates the translation to 1941, a period of intense creativity: many of the stories in *Ficciones* and *El Aleph*, as well as the essays collected in *Other Inquisitions*, date from that time.

Monegal argues that as a result of this translation, Faulkner's literature, "intense and baroque," became "naturalized" in Spanish, thus *easing* "its assimilation and adaptation in the pens of young narrators such as Juan Carlos Onetti (*Para esta noche*, 1943), Juan Rulfo (*Pedro Páramo*, 1955) and Gabriel García Márquez (*La mala hora* [Evil Hour], 1963)." Hence, the implication is made that *The Wild Palms*, in Borges's rendition, opened the door to Faulkner's mammoth influence over south-of-the-border literature at midcentury. This is true but not fully: the version by the Argentine did have a considerable impact, but by 1940 Faulkner was already a well-known figure in the Spanish-speaking world; among others, Lino Novás Calvo, the Cuban poet, had translated him into English (Calvo rendered *Sanctuary* in 1934).

But this translation was barely passable, as were several others. Borges, on the other hand, mimicked the American's style elegantly, making it fluid, electrifying, breathtaking in Spanish. Monegal argued: "[His] translation was not only faithful to the original but created in Spanish a writing style that was the equivalent of the original's English. For many young Latin American novelists who did not know enough English to read the dense original, Borges's tight version meant the discovery of a new kind of narrative writing. They had [in it] the best possible guide to Faulkner's dark and intense world."

A set of questions arise: How come Borges, at the time a tetragenarian of national prominence—not until 1961 was he awarded, along with Samuel Beckett, the International Publisher's Prize—decided to translate the author of *As I Lay*

Dying? And why embark on *The Wild Palms* specifically, a fairly mediocre title in Faulkner's corpus (the original title, changed by the American publisher, was *If I Forget Thee, Jerusalem* [Psalms 137:5])?

James Woodall, another one of Borges's biographers, suggests that, aside from the novel, the Argentine translated for Emecé Editores one or a handful of stories by Faulkner, although I've not seen them. What I have not only seen but scrutinized in detail are the Argentine's opinions on Faulkner. For the most part, he delivered them in the second half of the thirties, in three reviews he wrote for the Argentine magazine *El Hogar*: in order of appearance, on *The Unvanquished* (January 22, 1937); on *Absalom, Absalom*! (January 21, 1938); and on *The Wild Palms* (May 5, 1939).

In these commentaries he articulated his wholehearted admiration for the American: in a nutshell, he describes Faulkner as an author that doesn't attempt to explain his characters; instead, Borges portrayed him as one that shows us what they feel, how they act. I quote (in Spanish): "El mundo que imagina es tan real, que también abarca lo inverosímil." Of *Absalom! Absalom*! the Argentine announces that it possesses "an almost intolerable intensity" and equates it, in quality, to *The Sound and the Fury*: "I don't know if there's a higher praise," he concludes. In contrast, *The Wild Palms* strikes him as a lesser work, its technical novelties less attractive than uncomfortable, less justifiable than exasperating. He concludes (again, in Spanish): "Es verosímil la afirmación de que William Faulkner es el primer novelista de nuestro tiempo. Para trabar conocimiento de él, la menos apta de sus obras me parece The Wild Palms, pero incluye (como todos los libros de Faulkner) páginas de una intensidad que notoriamente excede las posibilidades de cualquier otro autor."

These quotes signal the degree to which Borges wasn't only familiar with English but had thoroughly internalized it. The style is English, and so is the *manner*. Notice I wrote manner, not mannerism: the former denotes measure; the latter denounces excess. Expressions such as "*Para trabar conocimiento*" and "*Es verosímil la afirmación*" are direct imports from expressions in Walt Whitman's tongue; translation: "To get acquainted with" and "It is feasible to affirm." But they are something else too: appropriations, reinventions. And so is the overall style of the sentences. *Verosímil* in particular, a Borgesian adjective, is infrequent in Spanish: its cognates might approach "accurate," "feasible," "realistic," and, at the suggestion of the *Oxford Spanish Dictionary*: "plausible."

Monegal is right: from Rulfo onward to Mario Vargas Llosa (and even to this day, to figures such as Ricardo Piglia), Faulkner remains an enormous literary influence in Latin America. But what inspired the majority of authors—the suffering, devastation, and defeat in the Deep South—did not attract Borges. What he saw in the author of *The Hamlet* is altogether different: a mastery of artifice, namely, a novelist devoted to recreating the inner life of his characters and to experimenting with the elasticity of the novel as a literary genre. It wasn't pain that the Argentine empathized with, but the *capability of turning it into the core of a self-contained parallel universe*. For him History, with a capital H, was less significant than the effects of literature on the reader. In his eyes, Faulkner was first and foremost a technician; that Yoknapatawpha is to be found in Mississippi is, I think, a sheer accident.

I imagine Borges in the late thirties, in need of money, sharing with Victoria Ocampo his willingness to translate from the English. She probably asked him who his choices were; he named Wilde, H. G. Wells, Stevenson, Melville, Kipling, Faulkner. The list prompted a series of business contacts on her part, and thus the list was reduced to a couple of concrete possibilities. In other words, I think it is less plausible that the Argentine selected *The Wild Palms* than the other way around. Upon its publication in the United States, Faulkner's novel was welcomed with scant enthusiasm. In *New Masses* (February 7,

1939), Edwin Berry Burgum wrote: "In his distinguished career, Mr. Faulkner has not written a more thoroughly satisfying novel than [this one]." But in the *Listener* (March 30, 1939), Edwin Muir dissented: "Mr. Faulkner's world of imagination is really a prolonged dream or rather a nightmare, into which civil functionaries from another dream intrude now and then; but the tortured inner eye cannot account for these people, for to it the ordinary is the sharpest surprise of all. Mr. Faulkner has flashes of genius . . . but his novel accounts for nothing."

The time has come to compare the originals by Faulkner in English and Borges in Spanish. I've opened at random *Novels 1936–1940*, edited by Joseph Blotner and Noel Polk (The Library of America, 1990). My eyes fall on pages 516 and 517:

> He had been in the hospital almost two years now. He lived in the intern's quarters with the others who, like him, had no private means; he smoked once a week now: a package of cigarettes over the week-end and he was paying the note which he had executed to his half sister, the one- and two-dollar money orders in reverse now, returning to source, the one bag would still hold all he owned, including his hospital whites—the twenty-six years, the two thousand dollars, the railroad tickets to New Orleans, the one dollar and thirty-six cents, the one bag in a corner of a barracks-like room furnished with steel army cots; on the morning of his twenty-seventh birthday he walked and looked down his body toward his foreshortened feet and it seemed to him that he saw the twenty-seven irrevocable years diminished and foreshortened beyond them in turn, as if his life were to lie passively on his back as though he floated effortless and without volition upon an unreturning stream. He seemed to see them: the empty years in which his youth had vanished—the years for wild

oats and for daring, for the passionate tragic ephemeral loves of adolescence, the girl- and boy-white, the wild importunate fumbling flesh, which had not been for him; lying so he thought, not exactly with pride and certainty not with the resignation which he believed, but rather with that peace with which a middleleaged eunuch might look back upon the dead time before his alteration, at the fading and (at last) edgeless shapes which now inhabited only the memory and not the flesh: *I have repudiated money and hence love. Not abjured it, repudiated. I do not need it; by next year or two years or five years I will know to be true what I now believe to be true: I will not even need to want it.*

Pages 37 and 38 of *Las palmeras salvajes*:

Hacía casi dos años que estaba en el hospital. Vivía en los pabellones de internos con otros que como él carecían de recursos particulares; fumaba una vez por semana, un atado de cigarrillos para el fin de semana, y estaba pagando la deuda que había reconocido a su propia hermana: los giros de uno o dos pesos que volvían ahora a su fuente de orígen; la única valija contenía aún todo lo que poseía, incluyendo sus uniformes blancos de hospital—sus 26 años, los 2.000 dólares, el billete de tren a Nueva Orleáns, el dólar 36 centavos en esa única valija, en el rincón de un caurto como un cuartel con camas militares de hierro en la mañana de su vigésimoséptimo cumpleaños. Se despertó y miró su cuerpo tendido hacia el escorzo de los pies y le pareció ver los veintisiete irrevocables años como disminuídos y escorzados detrás, como si su vida flotara sin esfuerzo y sin voluntad por un río que no vuelve. Le parecía verlos: los años vacíos en

> que había desaparecido su juventud—los años para la osadía y las aventuras, para los apasionados, trágicos, suaves, efímeros amores de la adolescencia, para la blancura de la muchacha y del muchacho, para la torpe, fogosa, importuna carne, que no había sido para él; acostado, pensaba, no exactamente con orgullo y no con la resignación que suponía, sino más bien con una paz de eunuco ya entrado en años que considerara el tiempo muerto que precedió a su alteración, que considerara las formas borrosas y (al fin) desdibujadas que sólo habitan en la memoria y no ya en la carne: *He repudiado el dinero y por consiguiente el amor. No abjurado, repudiado. No lo necesito; el año que viene o de aquí a dos años o cinco sabré que es cierto lo que ahora creo que es cierto: ni siquiera querré desearlo.*

The resemblance—in syntax, in spirit—is startling: Borges builds his text almost word by word; he compresses Faulkner subtly, but does so reproducing the cadence of the English version. His translation (in "The Translators of the *One-Thousand Nights*," perhaps symptomatically, he uses the term *traslación* in Spanish for translation) takes few *tangible* liberties; the riskiest *intangible* liberty it takes is to emulate Faulkner in Spanish by "readapting" Cervantes language to fit the needs. Indeed, he might have allowed, in Monegal's phrase, "the discovery of a new type of narrative." One might argue that the Argentine failed to give his translation any autonomy. But the autonomy is in it: silent, unobtrusive, unsettling the target tongue.

There are many approaches to translation. They might be reduced to two: The *Flaubertian Way*, in which the translator disappears without trace; and *The Nabokovian Way*, in which the translator endlessly stresses the artificiality of his endeavor. In *The Wild Palms* Borges endorses the first approach: he is *behind* Faulkner, not in front or at his side. His use of Italics, a prominent fixture in Faulkner (also, by the way, in the Argentine's own oeuvre), is exactly like the one in the English original; and the translator's footnotes he inserts are minimal: on page 27, for instance, he digresses: "*Old Man*: El Viejo: nombre familiar del río Misisipí"; another footnote explains the name *Jesse James*: "Léase los *Juan Moreira*, los *Hormiga Negra*, etc."

And on page 96, to the line "Drink up, ye armourous sons in a sea of hemingwaves," Borges states that the sentence is an example of "Retruécanos más bien intraducibles a la manera de James Joyce. *Armourous* = armour + amorous; *hemingwaves* = waves + Hemingway." And yet . . . For most people, the act of reading a work in a language other than the original is a way *into* another culture. But when the reader is acquainted with the original tongue, the act procures an altogether different meaning: it becomes an exercise of concordance. In spite of its resourcefulness, the Spanish version by Borges in my view isn't superior to its English counterpart. For a reader unfamiliar with Faulkner, *Las palmeras salvajes* is lucid, startling even; but the fact that the Argentine venerated the author of *The Wild Palms* and not the book itself is in display.

This brings me back to my original queries: Why is it so distressing to suggest that Borges in English feels like "at home"? And why does it infuriate that a translation might supersede its source? Because our approach to literature is filtered through the lens of malleable nationalist feelings. We enjoy claiming than an author, any author, is the sole property of an individual culture; that he or she could only have sprung from that culture and that his or her oeuvre holds the keys to understanding him or her. This view promotes the idea of human imagination as a series of loosely interrelated ghettos, each controlled by its own self-righteous inhabitants. But translation as an endeavor presupposes that no man is an island. It also proclaims that the only artist that is handcuffed is the one convinced that he is indeed an island onto his own.

It matters little if the Argentine, who is nobody's property, is read in French, Portuguese, English . . . , as long as the translations are enraptured by the same *zeitgeist* as his own Spanish versions.

Nota Bene: Years after a version of this chapter appeared in the volume *Look Away!: The U.S. South in New World Studies* (2004), edited by Jon Smith and Deborah Cohn, I was engaged in a conversation on it—and, specifically, on Borges's version of Faulkner's *The Wild Palms*—by Professor Charles Hatfield of the University of Texas at Dallas. It was part of a larger dialogue on translation as a fixture of Latin American culture from pre-Columbian times through the age of independence and modernization and up to the twenty-first century.

> Professor Hatfield: There are a number of mysteries surrounding Borges's translation of *The Wild Palms*—Douglas Day highlights some of them in his great essay called "Borges, Faulkner, and the Wild Palms" (*Virginia Quarterly Review*, Winter 1980), an essay that I love if only for having brought to my attention Alan Tate's description of Faulkner as a "Dixie Gongorist." Day also settles an important point: it's often said (for example, by Efraín Kristal in his book on Borges and translation, twenty years after Day's essay) that Borges sanitized Faulkner's text, when in fact, as Day points out, Borges was merely basing his translation on the already sanitized British edition of the novel published by Chatto and Windus in London.
>
> I won't repeat all the intricacies in Day's argument, but suffice it to say this: Borges wrote reviews of *Absalom! Absalom!*, *The Unvanquished*, and *The Wild Palms* in the journal *El Hogar* in the late 1930s, and while he had high praise for *Absalom* and *The Unvanquished*, with regard to *The Wild Palms* he

wrote that Faulkner's "technical novelties" seemed "less attractive than bothersome, less justifiable than exasperating." In the end, Borges suggested that the novel would not be a good introduction to Faulkner's writing. So why did he translate it? Day suggests that the reasons are pretty banal, having to do more with rights and publishing houses and contracts than with Borges's own choice. But the more interesting question has to do with why Borges seemed to attribute the translation to his mother many years later, and Day suggests that the importance of Borges's translation of *The Wild Palms* is that it occurs at a time when Borges was turning away "from the psychological experimentalism and brutal (one is tempted to say 'messy') content of a William Faulkner and turned to a form which for him rendered the novel redundant and irrelevant: *Ficciones*."

As to the translation, Day says that it is "good, very good." There's a lot of debate about Borges's translation, either in terms of whether it's good or bad, and what place it occupies in Borges's literary development (see Earl Fitz and his son Ezra Fitz's article, "Faulkner, Borges, and the Translation of *The Wild Palms*: The Evolution of Borges' Theory Concerning the Role of the Reader in the Game of Literature," in *Faulkner Journal* [Fall 2009], for an example). I recently came across a brief discussion of some other assessments of Borges's novel in Gareth Wood's book on Javier Marías and translation (which corrects Kristal's oversight of the British edition that Borges was working from). One is by Marías himself, who wrote that Borges translated Faulkner "*bastante mal*," adding that it was not "*por sus argentinismos, sino por su conocimiento imperfecto del inglés*" and also, more interestingly, because of his "*falta de aliento novelístico*." Wood looks carefully at both translations, and uncovers interesting renderings, such as, for example, when Borges translates "You're mad because he used a scalpel without having a diploma" as "*Te has enloquecido porque ha usado un bisturí sin tener diploma*," mistaking "mad" meaning "angry" for "mad" meaning "crazy." The other is by Juan Benet, who wrote in reference to Borges's edition that "*me veo obligado a transcribir las citas del texto traducido por Borges, por carecer de otra edición*." Wood himself calls parts of the translation, dialogue in particular, "flat and staid, attempting none of the verbal idiosyncrasies of popular speech." Then there is Piglia's claim that "*lo que uno encuentra en esa traducción es una lucha entre el estilo de Borges y el estilo de Faulkner*."

I recently had the pleasure of reading your essay, "Beyond Translation: Borges and Faulkner," which ends with a detailed analysis of Borges's translation of William Faulkner's *The Wild Palms*. You suggest that Borges's *ars poetica* of translation comes in four parts—his story "Pierre Menard, Author of the *Quixote*," his essays "On William Beckford's *Vathek*," and "The Translators of *The Thousand and One Nights*," and finally his own translation of Faulkner's *The Wild Palms*. You note that "the resemblance—in syntax, in spirit—is startling" between the two texts, and you go on to argue that if it can be said there are two approaches to translation (one in which the translator "disappears," and another in which "the translator endlessly stresses the artificiality of his endeavor"), Borges comes down on the side of the former. In his translation of *The Wild Palms*, Borges is "*behind* Faulkner, not in front or at his side."

Let's begin our discussion of Borges's translation of Faulkner, which raises a lot of questions and promises to be a long discussion, by asking you to revisit some of your claims. Later on, I want to ask you to say more about what you ultimately make of all of this—namely, the notion that Borges's translation leads us beyond "nationalist feelings" and towards a recognition of literature's global interrelatedness.

Ilan Stavans: I'm glad you've found the essay provocative. Translation is a cornerstone in oeuvre. *Menardismo*, as you know, has even become an ideology, just as *Quixotismo* is too. Borges translated lots of texts throughout his career. He started quite young, with Oscar Wilde. The translation was for a time mistakenly credited to his father. He also translated Virginia Woolf, for whom he had little patience as reader. In Buenos Aires magazines, he translated ghost stories, essays by G. K. Chesterton and Poe, and other stuff. As for Faulkner, he loved him, as did Onetti and García Márquez: because his Deep South was much like Latin America, a region scarred by history. Except that Borges didn't seek to rewrite Yoknapatawpha County; he simply savored it as reader.

Reading and translating are one and the same thing, for Borges and for myself. In his essay on Beckford's *Vathek*, he says that the original can be untruthful to the translation. And in his meditation on *The Thousand and One Nights*, he argues that translators have taken liberties that have gone beyond the semantic level, sometimes introducing, as in the case of Jean Antoine Galland, the precursor of Captain Richard Francis Burton and Edward Lane, among others, entirely new episodes and characters, as in the case of Sinbad.

Nabokov, in rendering Pushkin's *Eugene Onegin* into English, makes his version baroque, artificial. He abuses the footnote. His one-time friend Edmund Wilson attacked this Pushkin version rather viciously in the pages of the newly created *New York Review of Books*. Borges cannot escape his own semantics; he translates using adjectives the way only Borges would use them. (Remember the opening of "The Circular Ruins": "*Nadie lo vio desembarcar en la unánime noche*.") But he has no intension of upstaging Faulkner, at least not overtly.

Of course, it is important to notice, as you do, what Douglas Day argues: that Borges's primary source wasn't the original American but the expurgated English edition of Chatto and Windus. I don't believe I had read Day's *VQR* essay when I wrote my review in the *TLS*, nor when I meditated on it in my essay featured in *Look Away!* I've now read it. Day expand on the reasons why Borges took the job:

> The translation rights to *The Wild Palms* may have been bought by Borges' friend Victoria Ocampo for the publishing house, Sur. Those rights were then presumably transferred to Sudamericana, which had only just been founded. It is possible that the deal involving the transfer might have stipulated that Borges be the translator—not an unreasonable assumption, especially given Borges' prominent championing of Faulkner. It is also possible that Borges later wished to give the impression that his mother had done the translation, either wholly or in part, because it was a task undertaken primarily not for love of Faulkner, but for the fee paid the translator. It is more than likely, finally, that Borges' modesty about the attribution

> came as much as from anything else from his growing disenchantment with the novel as an art form, and more specifically with Faulkner as a practitioner of that form.

Borges's possible regret isn't surprising. I myself have gone through a particular project, and after seeing it in press, wished I had put my energy elsewhere.

Professor Hatfield: What fascinates me (and I don't want to seem like I'm avoiding talking about particular passages in the translation—we can do more of that if you'd like) is the attention that this translation by Borges has generated. It sounds like a weird question, but why do we care so much about Borges's *Las palmeras salvajes*? It can't just be, I think, because it was a text that was responsible in large part for introducing generations of Latin American writers to Faulkner, and it can't just be because we all love Borges and so we naturally are fascinated by his translations, right? In other words, I wonder if there's some anxiety getting worked out through all of this—an anxiety about the "originality" of the Latin American novel, or what it would mean if *el gran* Borges just did the translation (as Day sort of implies) for the cash, or about *translation* as an activity *writ large*. Maybe it's a stupid question, I'm still not sure, but I wonder what we're all getting when we argue that Borges *did it good* or *did it bad* or *made it his own* or *didn't make it his own* or *theorized through doing it*, etc. What do you think?

IS: Once again, I thank you for the intriguing context you've provided, which offers a more complete picture than the one I had when I wrote my essay on Borges and Faulkner. First, let me endorse the serendipitous argument. Biography is always written in hindsight, through the rear-view mirror. Yet life is never lived that way: it's always unpredictable, arbitrary, even chaotic. Borges was a master in the art of curating his own career. When we look at it, it seems consistent, coherent, straightforward to a degree that, frankly, is suspicious. We all take detours, don't we? We all get lost. We embark on projects that become dead-ends. Of course, a convincing career is always measured by the thread uniting the successful projects. Yet what happens with those that ended up in the dumpster? That Borges probably did the job for money seems too pedestrian, like when I was hired to write a how-to book for the Smithsonian: I needed money to pay my first child's diapers, plain and simple.

I like Ricardo Piglia's description of Borges's translation of *Las palmeras salvajes* as a boxing ring. Borges's false starts are fascinating. His incapacity to let Faulkner's style breathe is symptomatic of his own overwhelming *barroquismo*. Why is this rendition so controversial? I think you may have hit the nail on the head. Faulkner will end up becoming the patron saint for Rulfo, Onetti, García Márquez, and others, the father of the fractured, experimental novel. Yet Borges, at this point, is already dissing the novel as a literary genre. He finds it exhaustive, too malleable. He ridicules Dostoyevsky's *Crime and Punishment* for convincing the reader that a heinous crime is worth committing for moral reasons. Plus, this comes at a time when translation is increasingly taken seriously in Latin America. Some intellectuals embrace it as a worthy endeavor, not something to be thrown to the dogs.

More to your point: almost every translation by Borges, for better or worse, has generated rivers of ink.

Therein his role as the Moses of literary translation in the Spanish-language Americas. The Faulkner case is emblematic but so is his fragmentary version of *Leaves of Grass*, for instance. Should anyone care about all this? Not really. But then again, plenty of intellectual endeavors are, for all intents and purposes, useless—more like navel gazing than anything else. Still, people make careers (Borges among them) out of such innocuous exercises. The reason is simple: intellectuals, to justify their existence, need to find something to do at all times. This might be a relentless race, a futile effort. Yet if these debates don't take place, what should energy be spent in? Harvesting lettuce? Cleaning houses?[3]

PART V

ON THE LANGUAGE OF GHOSTS

There was no one inside him.

—"Everything and Nothing" (1960)

I once heard an interview with M. Night Shyamalan, who directed *The Sixth Sense* (1999), in which he made more than a passing comment about ghosts being different from humans in that they don't know they are dead. "Whereas each us of sees other people, ghosts don't see other ghosts," he stated. "They live a rather lonesome existence."

Of course, Shyamalan's point is neither provable nor disprovable.

I want to switch topics. A few days back, I happened upon a brief essay by Borges called "On Dubbing," in which he lambasts the then-recent Hollywood invention (the piece was written in 1945) of devising "monsters which combine the illustrious features of Greta Garbo with the voice of Aldonza Lorenzo." Borges calls the mechanism "a malignant artifice" (*un maligno artificio*). He asks, sarcastically, "How can we fail to profess our admiration for this painful prodigy, for these ingenious phono-visual anomalies?"[1]

I, too, dislike dubbing. In the Spanish-speaking world, it is an infrequent practice on the silver screen—except in Spain—

and, regrettably, a ubiquitous one on TV. My father, a stage actor whose yearly income often came from *telenovelas*, also practiced other forms of acting: advertising (in Mexico, for a while he was the face of Vodka Nicolai and Zest soap) and, bizarrely, dubbing. He did Hanna-Barbera cartoons as well as American movies. The appearance of an English-speaking caveman running his Spanish sentences like a *peladito*, or of a U.S. military commander stationed in Vietnam with an improbable guttural tick was disturbing. I don't want to venture into the realm of psychology. I will say that, at the very least, it forbade me from dutifully paying attention to plot because my whole self was concerned with being in on a secret: the caveman and the commander were one and the same. How large was Abraham Stavans's realm of influence? Where else might he show up?

So my phobia to dubbing has a reliable domestic source. I will never forget seeing *Manhattan* in Madrid when it first came out, in 1979, with Woody Allen parading an atrocious, if not incomprehensible, Castilian accent. On the small screen, I could watch *Star Trek* and *Lost in Space* in dubbed versions only, so I naturally became convinced that the language of astronauts and space aliens was the same one I heard on the street.

I have less aversion toward subtitles and, when attending a foreign film, I rarely think about the fact that I'm not only watching but, at the same time, I'm reading what is on the screen. In some strange way, Borges's teachings, inspired by Mallarmé and by the Kabbalists—that the universe is a book, not a movie, and that we are all characters in it—applies even to the moving image. I love foreign films, I love the experience of opening a window through them into another reality in which I'm an outsider; I love being perplexed by cultural patterns I'm unfamiliar with; I love not understanding the language; and I love being somewhat lost. But the world to me doesn't feel like a movie, it feels like a book, endless, unexplainable, written by an Author whose ultimate motifs we shall never understand.

As a citizen of the United States, I'm aware I'm in the minority among American moviegoers, since the appetite for subtitled features here constitutes a minuscule fraction of the overall annual box office. When a non–English language movie is—or is likely to be—successful, Hollywood producers quickly move to redo it, to domesticate it, as in the case of *The Girl with the Dragon Tattoo*.

Why are many Americans allergic to subtitles? Laziness, for starters. As a student of mine put it, "We go to the theater to enjoy, not to do homework." This allergy, of course, is evident in other aspects of life. In fact, foreign languages in general, whether in higher education or among immigrants, may be viewed with suspicion. The same student says, "Why doesn't the entire globe just learn English, and stop wasting energy and resources on the issue?" The empire is parochial. Its heart is shallow.

Although I'm used to them, subtitles, I must say, can be a malignant artifice, too. Punctilious as I am about language, I often get distracted when stumbling upon a typo, or worse, a mistake. These happen especially when subtitlers seem to come across some type of slang. The outcome is often humorous, for all the wrong reasons.

Quick: How do you say "*jíjole*" in English? Or "*épale*"? I forget what movie it was but not the mistake. One of the characters made a reference to a "*cholo chulo*": the subtitler opted for "handsome gangster," forgoing much more than an inspired alliteration. In another case (this one made in France), a woman tells her lover: "*lache-moi la grappe*." In puritanical mode, the subtitler resigned himself to a polite "Please leave!"

When a novel is rendered in another language, seldom is it featured side by side with the original (unlike poetry). Most readers, in other words, see the translation as an original. The translator, as a result, is freer. In contrast, because of the mechanics of subtitling, the translator is quasi naked before the public, since her work appears side by side with the original.

Borges, in "On Dubbing," wonders if, as part of evolution, "soon we will have to choose between watching dubbed films and not watching films at all." Seventy years later, the statement might sound falsely premonitory. However, with the monopoly of Hollywood movies, unabated for more than a century, it is important to keep in mind that Americans are an exception (they, and other English language speakers, enjoy their cinematic experience linguistically unadulterated), most people around the world see and read at the same time. Nobody, to my knowledge, complains: we are all resigned to a fate we aren't conscious of. After the Tower of Babel, there is really no other option.

In sum, I'm a devotee of this type of artifice. Actually, I am puzzled by how infrequently artists explore the endless possibilities of subtitles. In Israel in the eighties, a foreign movie could be shown with three lines of subtitles: Hebrew, English, and Arabic, with Russian either added or substituting for one of these languages. The effect was delicious if also maddening. Unhappily, such endeavor is now passé. (Arabic is seldom considered there. Jews and Arabs don't go to the movies together.)

On another plane, *Monty Python and the Holy Grail* (1975) starts by translating the credits into pidgin English-Swedish: "*Mønti Pythøn ik den Hølie Gräilen Røtern nik Akten Di Wik Alsø wik Alsø alsø wik Wi nøt trei a høliday in Sweden this yër?*" Plus, a new edition of the film has actual English subtitles, except that they come from Shakespeare's *Henry IV, Part 2* and, thus, have nothing to do with the plot.

In Europe, the same voice is always used in Meryl Streep or Tom Cruise movies. That means that a certain Italian actress or French actor *is* Streep in French and Cruise in Italian and not Streep and Cruise themselves. In those languages, these actors are reduced to a body.

Of course, Borges's interest in dubbing is part of a larger passion for language. In his essay "John Wilkins' Analytical Language" (*Other Inquisitions*), he devises an arbitrary language that, in the end, isn't more arbitrary than those we use every day anywhere on the globe. This paragraph was translated by Lilia Graciela Vázquez; edited by Jan Frederik Solem with assistance from Bjørn Are Davidsen and Rolf Andersen:

> He divided the universe in forty categories or classes, these being further subdivided into differences, which was then subdivided into species. He assigned to each class a monosyllable of two letters; to each difference, a consonant; to each species, a vowel. For example: *de*, which means an element; *deb*, the first of the elements, fire; *deba*, a part of the element fire, a flame. In a similar language invented by Letellier (1850) *a* means animal; *ab*, mammal; *abo*, carnivore; *aboj*, feline; *aboje*, cat; *abi*, herbivore; *abiv*, horse; etc. In the language of Bonifacio Sotos Ochando (1845) *imaba* means building; *imaca*, harem; *imafe*, hospital; *imafo*, pesthouse; *imari*, house; *imaru*, country house; *imedo*, coloumn; *imede*, pillar; *imego*, floor; *imela*, ceiling; *imogo*, window; *bire*, bookbinder; *birer*, bookbinding. (This last list belongs to a book printed in Buenos Aires in 1886, the "Curso de Lengua Universal," by Dr. Pedro Mata.)[2]

Just as Wilkins's language is a sophisticated ploy, so is Hollywood's invention of dubbing. It reminds me of yet another artifice. In his memoir *My Last Sigh* (1982), Luis Buñuel talks of an experiment, also devised by the American movie industry, to film the same film in the same set but in different languages geared toward specific audiences, each with its own native cast. *Dracula* (1931) with Bela Lugosi was thus shot during the day, with the Spanish language version done at night. The results are mesmerizing: paraphrasing Langston Hughes, *the same ain't ever the same*.

As stated before, Borges progressively lost his sight. It was a genetic curse: his father and grandfather also became blind around fifty; in other words, he knew this was his destiny. Intriguingly, in his oeuvre he seldom displays any interest in theater. Of movies, on the other hand, he was a devotee in his early life—until blindness took over. But maybe for a man who is progressively losing his sight, watching a foreign movie that is dubbed is better: you can at least follow the dialogue, whereas the subtitles are difficult to decipher.

Dubbing, subtitles, and the mischievous art of delivering a message by borrowing someone else's voice—these are variations on the translation process. I think of a ventriloquist, whose dummy is alive only when she lends it her modified voice. I am also reminded that in 1925, the Jewish philosophers Martin Buber and Franz Rosenzweig embarked on a new translation of the Bible into German. Their quest was to offer the sacred text to Jewish readers the way Martin Luther had offered his to Christian readers. Rosenzweig died a premature death in 1929; Buber toiled on alone, finishing it in 1961. In 1951, Gershom Scholem, the scholar of Kabbalah, who emigrated from Berlin to Jerusalem and thus escaped World War II, gave a speech to commemorate Buber's completion of the task. He stated: "Jews for whom you undertook this translation are no longer alive, and those among their children who escaped this catastrophe no longer read German."[3] What Scholem was referring to, I believe, is a disembodied readership, a phenomenon typical of languages without speakers. This is the case of languages such as Amurdag, Ubykh, Kamassian, Manx, Dalmatian, and Barbareño.

A friend of mine once told me about Manuel Segovia and Isidro Velázquez, from Ayapa, Mexico, considered to be the last speakers of Ayapaneco. But there was a feud between them and they refused to talk to each other.

As an outsider, Borges, I'm fully convinced, perceived himself as a ghost. That, at least, is the approach he offers about his ancestors in the essay "I, a Jew," in which he tried, in vain, to find his Jewish genealogical roots. And in his "Two English Poems," where he writes: "I offer you my ancestors my dead men, the ghosts that living men have honoured in marble: my father's father killed in the frontier in Buenos Aires, two bullets through his lungs, bearded and dead, wrapped by his soldiers in the hide of a cow; my mother's grandfather—just twenty-four—heading a charge of three hundred men in Peru, now ghosts on vanished horses." He himself was at once at home in Argentina as well as a foreigner.

This Borges learned from diaspora Jews, resilient specters that refuse to vanish, looping for millennia from one place to another. Jews as outsiders, apparitions, as wandering souls that, in their eternal pilgrimage, become free, that is, engagingly disengaged.

Wouldn't it be disquieting to be familiar with a never-released movie—let's imagine it a masterpiece—of which the only surviving item is not the movie itself, not even its script (its scene-by-scene denouement), but a plain and rather mechanical transcription of its subtitles? Reading it would be like eavesdropping on ghosts.

CODA

BORGES Y YO

> What's good no longer belongs to anyone, not even to the other, but to language or tradition.
>
> —"Borges and I" (1960)

To conclude, I want to talk about Borges and me. There are two ways to do it. The first is to reflect on his essay "Borges and I":

There isn't one but many Borgeses, as many as the readers he has and, also, as many as the languages he is rendered into. I, for one, have him, first and foremost, in Spanish, which, because it was his native language, is fixed and untouchable—that is, sacred. In my youth, I tried copying to exhaustion, even plagiarizing him. I also attempted to improve "The Secret Miracle," which I still think is perfect but for a line I believe was left out at the end. (My version, called "*Otro milagro secreto*," appears in *Prontuario* [Mexico: Joaquín Mortiz, 1988], 73–79.)

Aside from Spanish, I have him in Yiddish, English, Hebrew, German, French, Italian, Portuguese, Catalan . . . Reading him in these tongues is bizarre, like kissing a bride through a veil. He feels masked, though an occasional sentence is sometimes illuminating, to the degree of improving the original.

Not long ago, I embarked on a comparative reading, in my book *Quixote: The Novel and the World* (2015), of the twenty full-fledged versions of *Don Quixote of La Mancha* into English. Why that many? The answer is straightforward: language exists in a state of change. Indeed, its most constant aspect is that change. The first translation was into French. Then came the English one, of the First Part (1605), published in 1613, before the Second Part of the Cervantes's book was even released (1615). Its translator, Thomas Shelton, was, thus, also a dweller of the seventeenth century. His syntax is antiquated, difficult to follow today. That's why, with the work in the public domain, new versions are rushed into print. In spite of its youth, the twenty-first century alone is also fertile with its own translations, including one by Edith Grossman (2003), the only woman ever to embark on such a project.

Borges doesn't yet have a four-hundred-year-old history. Still, he is a favorite among translators, especially in English. (In part, that is due to his devotion to English and American literature. Also, to the fact that his first writings were in that language; intriguingly, his style in Spanish sometimes feels as if it has an English cadence to it.) There is a multiplicity of English versions—six, to be exact—of "*Borges y yo*," all of them, with one exception, called "Borges and I." The essay was published in *The Maker* (1960), when he was in his early sixties. Contrasting these versions is useful in understanding the ways the Argentine has traveled not only from one language to another but also within the English speaking world. The discrepancy between them might seem minuscule yet in a writer of Borges's caliber those nuances generate epistemological fractures.

They are presented in chronological order, according to their date of composition, and are preceded by the original. My purpose isn't to rank them—there is a turn of phrase, a different *no sé qué* I like in each of them—but, simply, to showcase the way translation becomes a cornucopia of possibilities: the same paragraph, perceived through a different prism. It befits Borges's compulsive bookishness. And it pays tribute to his view of Jewishness as an addiction to interpretation.

Al otro, a Borges, es a quien le ocurren las cosas. Yo camino por Buenos Aires y me demoro, acaso ya mecánicamente, para mirar el arco de un zaguán y la puerta cancel; de Borges tengo noticias por el correo y veo su nombre en una terna de profesores o en un diccionario biográfico. Me gustan los relojes de arena, los mapas, la tipografía del siglo XVIII, las etimologías, el sabor del café y la prosa de Stevenson; el otro comparte esas preferencias, pero de un modo vanidoso que las convierte en atributos de un actor. Sería exagerado afirmar que nuestra relación es hostil; yo vivo, yo me dejo vivir, para que Borges pueda tramar su literatura y esa literatura me justifica. Nada me cuesta confesar que ha logrado ciertas páginas válidas, pero esas páginas no me pueden salvar, quizá porque lo bueno ya no es de nadie, ni siquiera del otro, sino del lenguaje o la tradición. Por lo demás, yo estoy destinado a perderme, definitivamente, y sólo algún instante de mí podrá sobrevivir en el otro. Poco a poco voy cediéndolo todo, aunque me consta su perversa costumbre de falsear y magnificar. Spinoza entendió que todas las cosas quieren perseverar en su ser; la piedra eternamente quiere ser piedra y el tigre un tigre. Yo he de quedar en Borges, no en mí (si es que alguien soy), pero me reconozco menos en sus libros que en muchos otros o que en el laborioso rasgueo de una guitarra. Hace años yo traté de librarme de él y pasé de las mitologías del arrabal a los juegos con el tiempo y con lo infinito, pero esos juegos son de Borges ahora y tendré que idear otras cosas. Así mi vida es una fuga y todo lo pierdo y todo es del olvido, o del otro.

No sé cuál de los dos escribe esta página.[1]

I start with Anthony Kerrigan's rendition (1962). Kerrigan taught at Notre Dame and Indiana University. He also translated Pablo Neruda, Camilo José Cela, José Ortega y Gasset, and, prominently, Miguel de Unamuno's *Tragic Sense of Life in Men and in Peoples*:

> Things happen to him, the other one, to Borges. I stroll about Buenos Aires and stop, almost mechanically now perhaps, to look at the arch of an entranceway and the ironwork gate; news of Borges reaches me in the mail and I see his name on an academic ballot or in a biographical dictionary. I like hourglasses, maps, eighteenth-century typography, etymologies, the taste of coffee, and Robert Louis Stevenson's prose; he shares these preferences, but with a vanity that turns them into the attributes of an actor. It would be an exaggeration to say that our relationship is a hostile one; I live, I go on living, so that Borges may contrive his literature; and that literature justifies me. I do not find it hard to admit that he has achieved some valid pages, but these pages cannot save me, perhaps because what is good no longer belongs to anyone, not even to him, the other one, but to the language or to tradition. In any case, I am destined to perish, definitely, and only some instant of me may live on in him. Little by little, I yield him ground, the whole terrain, though I am quite aware of his perverse habit of magnifying and falsifying. Spinoza realized that all things strive to persist in their own nature: the stone eternally wishes to be stone and the tiger a tiger. I shall subsist in Borges, not in myself (assuming I am someone), and yet I recognize myself less in his books than in many others, or than in the intricate flourishes played on a guitar. Years ago I tried to free myself from him, and I went from the

> mythologies of the city suburbs to games with time and infinity, but now those games belong to Borges, and I will have to think up something else. Thus is my life a flight, and I lose everything, and everything belongs to oblivion, or to him.
>
> I don't know which one of the two of us is writing this page.[2]

I'm unconvinced by "I stroll about" or "I yield him ground, the whole terrain"; the verb *yield* makes me think of harvest.

Anyway, on to James E. Irby's 1964 rendition. Like Kerrigan, Irby was an academician. He taught at Princeton for decades. Along with Donald A. Yates, he introduced Borges to a large English language audience through the New Directions volume *Labyrinths*:

> The other one, the one called Borges, is the one things happen to. I walk through the streets of Buenos Aires and stop for a moment, perhaps mechanically now, to look at the arch of an entrance hall and the grillwork on the gate; I know of Borges from the mail and see his name on a list of professors or in a biographical dictionary. I like hourglasses, maps, eighteenth-century typography, the taste of coffee and the prose of Stevenson; he shares these preferences, but in a vain way that turns them into the attributes of an actor. It would be an exaggeration to say that ours is a hostile relationship; I live, let myself go on living, so that Borges may contrive his literature, and this literature justifies me. It is no effort for me to confess that he has achieved some valid pages, but those cannot save me, perhaps because what is good belongs not to one, not even to him, but rather to the language and tradition. Besides, I am destined

> to perish, definitely, and only some instant of myself can survive me. Little by little, I am giving over everything to him, though I am quite aware of his perverse custom of falsifying and magnifying things. Spinoza knew that all things long to persist in their being; the stone eternally wants to be a stone and the tiger a tiger. I shall remain in Borges, not in myself (if it is true that I am someone), but I recognize myself less in his books than in many others or in the laborious strumming of a guitar. Years ago I tried to free myself from him and went from the mythologies of the suburbs to the games with time and infinity, but those games belong to Borges now and I shall have to imagine other things. Thus my life is a flight and I lose everything and everything belongs to oblivion, or to him.
>
> I do not know which of us has written this page.[3]

The third translation is by Norman Thomas Di Giovanni (1972) and it is titled "Borges and Myself." It was done in collaboration with Borges. After meeting him in Cambridge, Massachusetts, Di Giovanni, an American of Italian descent, moved to Buenos Aires to work with him on translating various books for a multiple book contract with the United States publisher E. P. Dutton. It appears that, after shaping several versions of Borges's stories and essays in English, Di Giovanni persuaded him to change the original in order to mirror the translation. The strategy seems to me fraudulent: the translator becoming a tyrant, forcing the author to adapt to his wishes.

Borges's shyness is known to have resulted, in his adult age, in a docile, subdued personality. His blindness mostly placed him in the hands of others, acquaintances as well as strangers. According to Adolfo Bioy Casares's record of the period, Borges's friends, aware of the way Di Giovanni treated him, persuaded him to cease the relationship. One night, during supper while Bioy Casares was present, Borges got on the phone and finally told his translator off. Still, when Di Giovanni's maneuvers became known to the international community, a heated debate ensued on the role of translators in Borges's oeuvre. In this case, it was a translator who had also been doing the job of a literary agent, as Borges in his lifetime never had one to represent him.

At any rate, here is the rendition by Di Giovanni, with Borges's help:

> It's to the other man, to Borges, that things happen. I walk along the streets of Buenos Aires, stopping now and then—perhaps out of habit—to look at the arch of an old entranceway or a grillwork gate; of Borges I get news through the mail and glimpse his name among a committee of professors or a dictionary of biography. I have a taste for hourglasses, maps, eighteenth-century typography, the roots of words, the smell of coffee, and Stevenson's prose; the other man shares these likes, but in a showy way that turns them into stagy mannerisms. It would be an exaggeration to say that we are on bad terms; I live, I let myself live, so that Borges can weave his tales and poems, and those tales and poems are my justification. It is not hard for me to admit that he has managed to write a few worthwhile pages, but these pages cannot save me, perhaps because what is good no longer belongs to anyone—not even the other man—but rather to speech and tradition. In any case, I am fated to become lost once and for all, and only some moment of myself will survive in the other man. Little by little, I have been surrendering everything to him, even though I have evidence of his stubborn habit of falsification and exaggeration. Spinoza held that all things try to keep on being

> themselves; a stone wants to be a stone and the tiger a tiger. I shall remain in Borges, not in myself (if it is so that I am someone), but I recognized myself less in his books than in those of others or than in the laborious tuning of a guitar. Years ago, I tried ridding myself of him, and I went from myths of the outlying slums of the city to games with time and infinity, but those games are now part of Borges, and I will have to turn to other things. And so, my life is a running away, and I lose everything and everything is left to oblivion or to the other man.
>
> Which of us is writing this page I don't know.[4]

I find sudden poetry in "my life is a running away"—"*mi vida es una fuga.*"

Then comes Andrew Hurley's, and it was published in 1998. He also taught, in his case at the University of Puerto Rico. He translated works by Fray Bartolomé de Las Casas, Rubén Darío, Reinaldo Arenas, Ernesto Sábato, Heberto Padilla, and Ana Lydia Vega. It was Hurley who in the mid-nineties was chosen by Andrew Wylie, an agent for María Kodama, as well as the New York publisher Viking, to retranslate Borges, in part as a strategy to debunk, or at least eclipse, Di Giovanni's available translations:

> It's Borges, the other one, that things happen to. I walk through Buenos Aires and I pause—mechanically now, perhaps—to gaze at the arc of an entryway and its inner door; news of Borges reaches me by mail, or I see his name on a list of academics or in some biographical dictionary. My taste runs to hourglasses, maps, seventeenth-century typefaces, etymologies, the taste of coffee, and the prose of Robert Louis Stevenson; Borges shares those preferences, but in a vain sort of

way that turns them into the accouterments of an actor. It would be an exaggeration to say that our relationship is hostile—I live, I allow myself to live, so that Borges can spin out his literature, and that literature is my justification. I willingly admit that he has written a number of sound pages, but those pages will not save *me*, perhaps because the good in them no longer belongs to any individual, nor even to that other man, but rather to language itself, or to tradition. Beyond that, I am doomed—utterly and inevitably—to oblivion, and fleeting moments will be all of me that survives in that other man. Little by little, I have been turning everything over to him, though I know the perverse way he has of distorting and magnifying everything. Spinoza believed that all things wish to go on being what they are—stone wishes eternally to be stone, and tiger, to be tiger. I shall endure in Borges, not in myself (if, indeed, I am anybody at all), but I recognize myself less in his books than in many others', or in the tedious strumming of a guitar. Years ago I tried to free myself from him, and moved on from the mythologies of the slums and outskirts of the city to games with time and infinity, but those games belong to Borges now, and I shall have to think up other things. So my life is a point-counterpoint, a kind of fugue, and a falling away—and everything winds up being lost to me, and everything falls into oblivion, or into the hands of the other man.

I am not sure which of us it is that's writing this page.[5]

More than a bit cumbersome, even baroque: "Beyond that, I am doomed—utterly and inevitably—to oblivion, and fleeting moments will be all of me that survives in that other man." Di Giovanni's syntax is, on occasion, fruitlessly ornate.

The next version, of 1999, is by Kenneth Krabbenhoft. He taught at New York University and also translated Neruda, St. John of the Cross, and Eugenio Trías:

> The other one. Borges, is the one things happen to. I wander around Buenos Aires, pausing perhaps unthinkingly, these days, to examine the arch of an entranceway and its metal gate. I hear about orgs in letters, I see his name on a roster of professors and in the biographical gazetter. I like hourglasses, maps, eighteenth-century typeface, the taste of coffee, and Stevenson's prose. The other one likes the same things, but his vanity transforms them into theatrical props. To say that our relationship is hostile would be an exaggeration: I live, I stay alive, so that Borges can make his literature, and this literature is my justification. I readily admit that a few of his pages are worthwhile, but these pages are not my salvation, perhaps because good writing belongs to no one in particular, not even to my other, but rather to language and tradition. As for the rest, I am fated to disappear completely, and only a small piece of me can possibly live in the other one. I'm handing everything over to him bit by bit, fully aware of his nasty habit of distortion and aggrandizement. Spinoza knew that all things desire to endure in their being: stones desire to be stones, and tigers tigers, for all eternity. I must remain in Borges rather than in myself (if in fact I am a self), and yet I recognize myself less in his books than in many others, or in the rich strumming of a guitar. Some years ago I tried to get away from him: I went from suburban mythologies to playing games with time and infinity. But these are Borges's games now—I will have to think of something else.

> Thus my life is an escape. I will lose everything, and everything will belong to oblivion, or to the other.
>
> I don't know which of us wrote this.[6]

"Biographical gazetter?" Each translator (no women here yet) reshapes Borges according to his own conception of language, his linguistic and biographical background. The body remains; the custom is different.

Now my own version of "Borges and I," included in *The FSG Book of Twentieth-Century Latin American Poetry* (2011):

> The other one, Borges, is to whom things happen. I walk through Buenos Aires, stop, maybe a bit mechanically, to look at an arch of an entrance way and a grillwork door; I have news from Borges by mail or when I see his name in a list of professors or in a biographical dictionary. I like hourglasses, maps, 18th-century typography, the taste of coffee, and Stevenson's prose; the other shares those preferences but with a vanity that turns them into an actor's attributes. It would be an exaggeration to affirm that our relationship is hostile; I live, I let myself live, so that Borges can plot his literature and that literature justifies me. It doesn't cost me anything to confess he has achieved a few valid pages, but those pages can't save me, perhaps because what's good no longer belongs to anyone, not even to the other, but to language or tradition. In any case, I'm destined to be lost, definitively, and just some instant of me will survive in the other. Little by little I cede everything, even though I'm aware of his perverse tendency to falsify and pontificate. Spinoza understood that all things want to be preserved in their being: the stone

> eternally wants to be a stone and the tiger a tiger. I shall remain in Borges, not in myself (if I am someone), but I recognize myself less in his books than in many by others and in the laborious strumming of a guitar. Years ago I tried freeing myself from him and went from the mythologies of the *arrabal* to the games with time and the infinite, but those games are Borges' now and I shall come up with other things. Thus my life is a flight and I lose everything and everything belongs to oblivion, or to the other.
>
> I don't know which of the two writes this page.[7]

After much effort, the line "*No sé cuál de los dos escribe esta página*" still sounds better in Spanish.

Ought the translator become invisible? Should the translation make the reader forget that what is at hand is a foreign artifact? As I mentioned before, the answer results in two approaches: one is to make the reader forget the original, to create the illusion that the rendition into the target language is the door—maybe even the sole entryway—to entering the writer's mind; the other is to remind the reader of the artifice that translation isn't a mere substitute for the original but its replacement.

In any case, these versions were produced within a span of fifty years. Language didn't change dramatically in that period. The deviations are thus due to style, fancifulness, and maybe individual understanding. All the translators are American save one, who is Mexican. Having six makes English a richer language in Borgesian possibilities than Spanish, where readers only have one version, although that is *the* version: sacrosanct, age-less. That original no longer belongs to Borges but to language and tradition.

Seen together, these translations convince me, yet again, that what makes classics inexhaustible is their multiplicity in another language and that approaching them in a single rendition is a form of impoverishment. Two, three, and more versions offer a kaleidoscope of interpretation. For in the end, any piece of writing isn't really one but many, as many—and as multifaceted—as its numerous readers.

The second way to engage with "Borges and I" is to literally talk about Borges and me, which is a suitable place to indulge in autobiography and, fittingly, to conclude this volume:

On June 16, 1986, the day after Borges died, I was in Buenos Aires. I had saved enough money to buy myself a plane ticket to Argentina, hoping to visit him. The purpose of my journey was far more ambitious: to acquaint myself with Jewish life in the Southern Cone. But in my eyes, Borges, in spite of his not being Jewish, was the epicenter of that life. Throughout his career, he had written admirable pieces on Kafka, Spinoza, and the Golem. He had visited Israel to receive the Jerusalem Prize and had identified with the youthful Jewish state in its struggle for existence in an unwelcoming Middle East. Far more important, his sensibility was Jewish: his inexhaustible memory; his passion for reading; his commitment to the treacherousness of translation; his ever-expanding polyglotism; and his understanding that cosmopolitanism, not nationalism, is the only panacea to the malaise of modern life.

Like most admirers, I knew that the prior November Borges had been diagnosed with cancer of the liver. But unbeknownst to me was the fact that he, along with María Kodama, his forty-year-old former student and now eight-weeks-old wife, had moved to Geneva. In my youthful mind—I had turned twenty-five in April—Borges was immortal. No other author, dead and alive, had influenced me more profoundly. I knew his oeuvre almost as if I had written it myself. I could recite his poems "Emerson," "General Quiroga Rides to His Death in a Carriage," "To Whoever Is Reading Me," and "The Moon." After nights of scrutinizing their actions, I had made his protagonists Pierre Menard, Erik Lönrrot, Jaromir Hladík, Emma Zunz, and the magus in "The Circular Ruins," close friends of mine, to the point of holding conversations with them. His essay "The Argentine Writer and Tradition," which I mentioned in the prologue, was written as a response of sorts to T. S. Eliot's "Tradition and the Individual Talent," and, as I saw it, was a manifesto: no artist, it stated, should be confined to the landscape in which he came of age. That landscape is a trampoline, not a prison.

It was thus a surprise when, upon walking to a newspaper kiosk in the corner of Calles Suipacha and Corrientes, near the modest Buenos Aires hotel I was stayed in, I read the loud headlines: *Borges muere en Ginebra.* He had passed away the morning prior in Geneva, Switzerland—purposely far away from home, since he was distraught with Argentina, a country that, at the end of the twentieth century, seemed more parochial than ever. My desire to connect with him was misguided. Some years earlier, I had attended a couple of events of his in Mexico (one at the Ollín Yollitzli Auditorium, in which he shared the stage, if I remember accurately, with Allen Ginsberg, Octavio Paz, and Günter Grass, among others), and, on an earlier visit to Buenos Aires, walked the street with him and visited his apartment.

Not this time . . . As I walked around retracing his path, in tribute to him, while reciting to myself lines of his work I had memorized ("*Yo camino por Buenos Aires y me demoro, acaso ya mecánicamente, para mirar el arco de un zaguán y la puerta cancel; de Borges tengo noticias por el correo y veo su nombre en una terna de profesores o en un diccionario biográfico*"), I realized that Borges's death was also my beginning. It is only so much that a young writer might bear when it comes to recognizing the impact of his predecessors on him. Maybe I needed to forget his oeuvre, to distance myself, to become free. Surely I had tried before. Years later, I chronicled my odyssey this way in my memoir, *On Borrowed Words*, written during a year-long stay in London:

> When I began to write, Borges had a decisive influence. His pure, precise, almost mathematical style; his intelligent plots; his abhorrence of *verborrea*—the overflow of words without end or reason, still a common malady in Spanish literature today. He, more than anyone before (including the *modernista* poet from Nicaragua, Rubén Darío), had taught a lesson: literature ought to be a conduit for ideas. But his lesson was hard to absorb, if only because Hispanic civilization is so unconcerned with ideas, so irritable about debate, so disinterested in systematic inquiry. Life is too rough, too unfinished to be wasted on philosophical disquisition. It is not by chance, of course, that Borges was an Argentine. It couldn't have been otherwise, for Argentina perceives itself—or rather, it *used to* perceive itself—as a European enclave in the Southern Hemisphere. Buenos Aires, its citizens would tell you in the 1940s, is the capital of the world, with Paris as a provincial second best.
>
> As soon as I discovered Borges, I realized, much as others have, that I had to own him. I acquired every edition I could put my hands on, not only in Spanish but in their French, English, Italian, German, and Hebrew translations, as well as copies of the Argentine monthly Sur, where his best work was originally featured, and interviews in journals. My collection began to grow as I embarked on my own first experiences in literature: tight descriptions, brief stories, passionless literary essays. Rather quickly the influence he exerted on me became obvious. In consolation, I would paraphrase for myself the famous line from "Decalogue of the Perfect Storyteller"—in

Spanish its title is infinitely better: "*Decálogo del perfecto cuentista*"—by Horacio Quiroga, a celebrated if tragic turn-of-the-century Uruguayan author: to be born, a young writer should *imitate* his beloved masters as much as possible. The maxim, I realize today, is not without dangerous implications; it has encouraged derivativeness and perhaps even plagiarism in Latin American letters. But I was blind to such views. My only hope as a litteratuer was not to be like Borges, but to *be* Borges. How absurd that sounds now!

Influence turned into anxiety, and anxiety into discomfort. Would I ever have my own voice? One desperate afternoon, incapable of drafting a single line I could call my own, I brought down all the Borges titles I owned, piled them in the garage, poured gasoline over them, and set them on fire. It was a form of revenge, a sacramental act of desperation: the struggle to be born, to own a place of one's own, to be like no one else—or, at least, unlike Borges. The flames shot up at first, and eventually, slowly, died down. I saw the volumes, between fifty and seventy in total, turn bright, then brown, then become ash. I smiled, thinking, in embarrassment, of Hitler's Germany, Pinochet's Chile, and Mao's China. I thought of Elias Canetti's *Auto-da-Fé* and Ray Bradbury's *Fahrenheit 451*. I thought of scores of prayer books, Talmuds, and other rabbinical works burnt by the Holy Inquisition in Spain and the New World, in places not far from my home. And I also invoked Borges' own essay, "The Wall and the Books," about Shih Huang Ti, the first emperor of China, a contemporary of Hannibal, whose reign was marked by the construction of the Wall of China, and also by the campaign to burn all history books. Shih Huang Ti saw himself as a new beginning. History needed to start over.[8]

Heinrich Heine said: "Wherever they burn books they will also, in the end, burn human beings." After the book burning, my infatuation, I confess, was left intact. Within a few months of my arrival to the United States, I already had acquired inexpensive English translations of various volumes, *Ficciones* among them. In fact, reading Borges in Shakespeare's tongue was a revelation. Since he had been close to English from an early age, it appeared to me (it still does) that his oeuvre is written in Spanish through the filter of English. That is, it feels as if it was conceived in one language but executed in another. The effect is stunning: the art of translation is in its DNA, even when it doesn't address the topic in upfront fashion. As a Mexican in New York with only sparse knowledge of *el inglés*, yet hoping not to become a pariah, an appendix, delving into Borges's writing using the words of my new habitat was comforting. It granted me a refuge, an opportunity to feel at home away from my native home.

I had been born into a Jewish household. My parents were children of immigrants from the Pale of Settlement (Poland, Belarus, and Ukraine). My first languages were Yiddish and Spanish. In my youth, I had fervently rebelled against my Jewish education, which felt parochial. I wanted to be a citizen of the world, not of a little house in the southern part of Mexico City. I burnt by vessels, traveling to Europe, Northern Africa, and the Middle East. I wanted little to do with being *un judío* and *un mexicano*. Since I dreamed of becoming a writer, I wrote incessantly, looking for my own voice.

Voice in literature is inevitably attached to place. The more we dream of the universe, the clearer and more significant our own immediately landscape becomes. My journeys brought me back home because home is where one's doubts originated. I was ashamed—maybe the right term is "terrified"—that I didn't love Mexico enough, that I could leave it in order to find answers elsewhere. And I was ashamed that my education hadn't made me fully Jewish, for if it had, why was I questioning my heritage?

I hadn't been a voracious reader before my departure. Upon returning, I sought answers in books. Eventually I found Borges. At first I felt repelled: he was too arrogant, too egotistical. Yet wasn't I too? I found his stories on *compadritos*, *orilleros*, and Tango personae contrived; I preferred his explorations of time and the infinite. Then it dawned on me: the two were sides of the same coin. Borges delved into his own milieu to understand his own heritage and he placed that heritage in a larger scale. It was stumbling across "The Argentine Writer and Tradition" that I finally came to understand him, or at least had the illusion of it. My recognition of my own place in the world came when he writes that Jews feel an almost religious devotion to culture because they "do not feel bound" by any devotion to that culture.

I indeed didn't feel bound by my either my Jewishness or my Mexicanness. Borges taught me this was fine. Actually, he showed me it was an advantage: not to feel bound is to be free.

Me sentí libre, I was free. I could now be Mexican and Jewish by choice, not by force. I repeat a few lines from Borges's essay that I have already quoted. In them he talks as an Argentine: "I believe our tradition is all of Western culture, and I also believe we have a right to that tradition, greater than that which the inhabitants of one or another Western nation might have." He adds: "I believe that we Argentines, we South Americans in general . . . can handle all European themes, handle them without superstition, with an irreverence which can have, and already does have, fortunate consequences." His conclusion is remarkable: "Anything we Argentine writers can do successfully will become part of our Argentine tradition, in the same way that the treatment of Italian themes belongs to the tradition of England through the efforts of Chaucer and Shakespeare."

Yes, anything I do successfully belongs to me as well as to the world's tradition. Defeat plays an essential part in literature: one needs to start by recognizing how fragile, how limited one's own viewpoint is. Yet there is contentment in defeat. I don't need to write in order to be part of a club; my work, if it has any merit, shall make the confines of that club less constraining, more elastic. That's because my own tradition is the world's tradition. Nothing should be strange to me: I shouldn't feel like an alien anywhere. Years later, I came across a line by Robert Louis Stevenson that ratified this belief and became a kind of mantra: "There is no foreign land; it is the traveler only who is foreign."

I owed Borges my gratitude. I wanted to meet him. I had seen him a couple of times in Mexico in large events and didn't have the time to talk to him in detail. So I sought him out in Buenos Aires . . . but arrived too late.

When I found out that he was no longer in and of this world, I let myself loose in Buenos Aires, teary-eyed, wandering—and wondering—without goal through city streets, retracing my affinity with the master, contemplating my own future as a novice, realizing my dialogue with him would forever be a private affair.

His work has been a map for me. It might seem ironic that a non-Jew would teach a Jew to recognize his own heritage. But isn't that what we Jews have always done, shaping our sense of self according to the needs of the environment? (Jean-Paul Sartre's slim book *Anti-Semite and Jew* (1946) comes to mind, in which the French philosopher argues, polemically, that Jews need anti-Semites to be themselves and vice versa.) Borges was my rabbinical master in a Yeshiva the size of the globe, and I his tentative pupil.

Borges y yo: I owe him my own voice.

ACKNOWLEDGMENTS

The foundations of this book dates back to 1986, when I was invited to deliver three lectures at the Jewish Theological Seminary under the title *Borges and the Jews*. Those lectures were eventually released, as an e-book, by the International Raoul Wallenberg Foundation.

Over the years, I have returned to the material time and again, alone and with others. I have continued to lecture on the topic in institutions in Argentina, England, Israel, Spain, and the United States, every time finding a different motif, a new twist. My meditations have also been nurtured in the classroom at Amherst College with a cadre of superb students.

The friends and colleagues whose viewpoints I have benefited from along the way are too numerous to list. However, I need to mention a handful—in alphabetical order—whose involvement was particularly significant in expanding my horizon and sharpening my arguments: Marcos Aguinis, Edna Aizenberg, Jaime Alazkari, Marcelo Birmajer, Marcelo Brodsky, Debora Cohen, Morris Dickstein, Norman Thomas Di Giovanni, Lindsay Duguid, Blake Eskin, Evelyn Fishburne, Laurence Goldstein, Jorge J. E. Gracia, Charles Hatfield, Andrew Hurley, Moshe Idel, Steven T. Katz, John King, S. Lillian Kremer, Alfred MacAdam, James Maraniss, Michael Millman, Alana Newhouse, Jonathan Rosen, Anthony Rudolph, David G. Roskies, Stephen A. Sadow, Neal Sokol, Alex Star, Mike Vázquez, Eliot Weinberger, Jason Wilson, Karen Winkler, Donald A. Yates, and Eric Zinner. In Tel-Aviv, Eliezer Nowodworski sent me a PDF of the Yiddish translation of Borges's work. It was edited by his grandfather, the *hombre de letras* Samuel Rollansky (aka Shmuel Rozhanski) for YIVO (aka IWO) in Buenos Aires. I appreciate the support of Yitskhok Niborski at the Maison de la culture Yiddish: Bibliotèque Medem in Paris. Laurie D. Searl was meticulous in shepherding the manuscript through production. And Neal Sokol prepared the index.

Some of these pages appeared, in somewhat different form, in the following periodicals: *Zeek*, *The Chronicle of Higher Education*, *The Forward*, *Jewish Review of Books*, *Jewish Quarterly*, *Modern Judaism*, *Michigan Quarterly Review*, *Prooftexts*, the *Times Literary Supplement*, and *Transition*. The chapter "Beyond Translation" appeared in *Look Away!: The U.S. South in New World Studies* (Duke University Press, 2004), edited by Jon Smith and Deborah Cohn. Earlier meditations of mine on Borges appear in my books *Tropical Synagogues* (Holmes and Meier, 1994), *The Inveterate Dreamer: Essays and Conversations on Jewish Culture* (University of Nebraska Press, 2001), *Ilan Stavans: Eight Conversations*, by Neal Sokol (University of Wisconsin Press, 2004), *Singer's Typewriter and Mine: Reflections on Jewish Culture* (University of Nebraska Press, 2012), and *Oy, Caramba: An Anthology of Jewish Stories from Latin America* (University of New Mexico Press, 2016). My gratitude to Charles Hatfield for the enlightening tête-à-tête on Borges's rendition of Faulkner's *The Wild Palms*.

Beth Bouloukos at SUNY Press encouraged me to turn the essays, lectures, conversations, and classroom notes into a volume. The result is this volume, mercifully more succinct that the countless reiterations I have engaged in over the years. All infelicities are mine alone.

Borges's oeuvre is collected in Spanish in three hefty volumes, *Obras Completas*, published by Emecé in Buenos Aires in 1967, and revised in 1974, 1989, and 1996. Various translations into English, of disparate quality, done by numerous individuals, are available. The most comprehensive, unified selection is the three volume set published by Viking in the United States, upon which I've drawn substantially in *Borges and the Jews*. It is comprised of *Collected Fictions*, translated by Andrew Hurley

(1998), as well as *Selected Poems*, edited by Alexander Coleman (1999), and *Selected Non-Fictions*, edited by Eliot Weinberger (both 1999).

Biographies of the Argentine have multiplied in the last several decades. I made substantial use of those by Marcos-Ricardo Barnatán (*Borges: Biografía total*, Temas de Hoy, 1995), Emir Rodríguez Monegal (*Jorge Luis Borges: A Literary Biography*, E. P. Dutton, 1978), Horacio Salas (*Borges: Una biografía*, Planeta, 1994), María Esther Vázquez (*Borges: Esplendor y derrota*, Tusquets, 1996), James Woodall (*Borges: A Life*, Basic Books, 1996), and Edwin Williamson (*Borges: A Life*, Viking, 2004). And I also found resourceful the interviews compiled in *Borges el memorioso* with Antonio Carrizo (Fondo de Cultura Económica, 1982) and the two volumes by Richard Burgin: *Conversations with Jorge Luis Borges* (Holt, Rinehart and Winston, 1969) and *Jorge Luis Borges: Conversations* (University Press of Mississippi, 1998).

Needless to say, I'm not the first to tackle the issue of Borges's relationship with the Jews. A number of scholarly studies have paved my way and upon which I've drawn in the preceding pages, among them *The Aleph Weaver: Biblical, Kabbalistic and Judaic Elements in Borges* (Scripta Humanistica, 1984), by Edna Aizenberg, as well as a couple of other books by Aizenberg: *Borges and his Successors: The Borgesian Impact on Literature and the Arts* (University of Missouri Press, 1990) and *Books and Bombs in Buenos Aires: Borges, Gerchunoff, and Argentine-Jewish Writing* (University Press of New England, 2002); Jaime Alazraki's *Borges and the Kabbalah and Other Essays on His Fiction and Poetry* (Cambridge University Press, 1988); Naomi Lindstrom's *Jewish Issues in Argentine Literature: From Gerchunoff to Szichman* (University of Missouri Press, 1989), and Saúl Sosnowski's *Borges y la Cábala: La búsqueda del verbo* (Pardés Ediciones, 1986).

Finally, the study of Borges's oeuvre I'm most fond of is *Jorge Luis Borges: A Writer on the Edge*, by Beatriz Sarlo, edited by John King (Verso, 1993). It analyzes him as the ultimate outsider, one that manages not only to reposition himself at center stage but to shift the place where that center is located.

NOTES

PART I. YO, JUDÍO

1. "An Autobiographical Essay," in *The Aleph and Other Stories: 1933–1969*, trans. Norman Thomas Di Giovanni, in collaboration with the author (New York: Dutton, 1972), 210–60.

2. "I, a Jew," trans. Eliot Weinberger, in *Selected Non-Fictions*, ed. Eliot Weinberger (New York: Viking, 1999), 110–11.

3. "Song to Argentina," trans. Ilan Stavans, introduction to *Rubén Darío: Selected Writings*, ed. Ilan Stavans (New York: Penguin Classics, 2005), XII.

4. Alberto Gerchunoff, "Camacho's Wedding Feast," trans. Prudencio de Pereda, in *Tropical Synagogues: Short Stories by Jewish–Latin American Writers*, ed. Ilan Stavans (New York and London: Holmes and Meier, 1994), 41–49.

5. Naomi Lindstrom, *Jewish Issues in Argentine Literature: From Gerchunoff to Szichman* (Columbia: University of Missouri Press, 1989), 57–58.

6. Leonardo Senkman, *La identidad judía en la literatura argentina* (Buenos Aires: Pardés, 1983), 72–73.

7. "Unworthy," trans. Andrew Hurley, in *Collected Fictions* (New York: Viking, 1998), 352–57.

8. "Emma Zunz," trans. Andrew Hurley, in *Collected Fictions*, 215–19.

9. Edna Aizenberg, *The Aleph Weaver: Biblical, Kabbalistic, and Judaic Elements in Borges* (Potomac, MD: Scripta Humanistica, 1984), 96.

10. "Blindness," trans. Eliot Weinberger, in *Selected Non-Fictions*, 482–83.

PART II. DEUTSCHES REQUIEM

1. "A Pedagogy of Hatred," trans. Suzanne Jill Levine, in *Selected Non-Fictions*, 199–201.

2. "Definition of a Germanophile," trans. Suzanne Jill Levine, in *Selected Non-Fictions*, 203–205.

3. "A Comment on August 23, 1944," trans. Suzanne Jill Levine, in *Selected Non-Fictions*, 210–11.

4. "*Deutsches Requiem*," trans. Andrew Hurley, in *Collected Fictions*, 229–34.

5. "The Argentine Writer and Tradition," trans. Esther Allen, in *Selected Non-Fictions*, 420–27.

PART III. A CATALOG OF JEWISH SYMBOLS

1. "The Golem," trans. Alan S. Trueblood, in *Selected Poems*, ed. Alexander Coleman (New York: Viking, 1999), 192–97.

2. Jaime Alazraki, *Borges and the Kabbalah and Other Essays on His Fiction and Poetry*. Cambridge: Cambridge University Press, 1988.

3. "A Defense of the Kabbalah," trans. Eliot Weinberger, in *Selected Non-Fictions*, 83–86.

4. "The Aleph," trans. Norman Thomas Di Giovanni, in *The Aleph and Other Stories: 1933–1969*, 15–30.

5. "Spinoza," trans. Willis Barnstone, in *Selected Poems*, 229.

6. "Baruch Spinoza," trans. Willis Barnstone, in *Selected Poems*, 383.

7. "Artifices: Foreword," trans. Andrew Hurley, in *Collected Fictions*, 129–30.

8. "Death and the Compass," trans. Andrew Hurley, in *Collected Fictions*, 147–56.

9. "Kafka and His Precursors," trans. Eliot Weinberger, in *Selected Non-Fictions*, 363–65.

10. Ibid., 501–503.

11. "The Secret Miracle," trans. Andrew Hurley, in *Collected Fiction*, 157–62.

12. Ilan Stavans,"Agnon: Borges' Invention," *The Jewish Daily Forward*, February 6, 2004.

13. "An Autobiographical Essay," in *The Aleph and Other Stories: 1933–1969*, trans. Norman Thomas Di Giovanni, in collaboration with the author (New York: Dutton, 1970), 2010–260.

14. Ilan Stavans, "Borges and Israel: Three Poems," in *Singer's Typewriter and Mine: Reflections on Jewish Culture* (Lincoln: University of Nebraska Press, 2013), 138–41.

15. "Isaac Babel," in *Obras Completas*, vol. IV: Biografías sintéticas (Buenos Aires: Emecé Editores, 2007), 415–16. My translation.

PART IV. BEYOND TRANSLATION

1. "Two English Poems," in *Obras Completas*, vol. II, 239–40.
2. "The Argentine Writer and Tradition," trans. Esther Allen, in *Selected Non-Fictions*, 420–27.
3. Ilan Stavans and Charles Hatfield Jr., "Silence is Meaningful," *The Buenos Aires Review*; http://www.buenosairesreview.org/2015/07/silence-is-meaningful/.

PART V. ON THE LANGUAGE OF GHOSTS

1. "On Dubbing," trans. Suzanne Jill Levine, in *Selected Non-Fictions*, 262–63.
2. "John Wilkins' Analytical Language," trans. Eliot Weinberger, in *Selected Non-Fictions*, 229–32.
3. Martin Buber, "Towards a New German Translation of Scriptures" ("Zu einer Neuen Verdeutschung der Schrift"), *Die Schrift*, vol. 1 (Berlin: Gebundene Ausgabe, 1954).

CODA

1. Jorge Luis Borges, *Obras Completas*, vol. II: 1952–1972 (Buenos Aires, Emecé, 1989), 186.
2. Borges, *A Personal Anthology*, trans. Anthony Kerrigan (New York: Grove, 1962), 200–201.
3. Borges, *Labyrinths: Selected Stories and Other Writings*, ed. Donald A. Yates and James E. Irby, trans. James E. Irby (New York: New Directions, 1964), 246–47.
4. "Borges and Myself," trans. Norman Thomas Di Giovanni, in *The Aleph and Other Stories, 1933–1969*, 151–52.
5. "Borges and I," trans. Andrew Hurley, in *Collected Fictions*, 324.
6. "Borges and I," trans. Kenneth Krabbenhoft in *Selected Poems*, 93.
7. Ilan Stavans, ed., *The FSG Book of Twentieth-Century Latin American Poetry* (New York: Farrar, Straus, and Giroux, 2011), 186–89.

8. Ilan Stavans, *On Borrowed Words: A Memoir of Language* (New York: Viking, 2001).

INDEX